The ESSENTIALS® of
REGISTERED TRADEMARK

COMPUTER SCIENCE I

Randall Raus, M.S.
Computer Engineer and
Computer Science Consultant
Seal Beach, CA

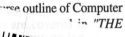

This book covers the ~~~~urse outline of Computer
Science I. Continu~~~~ ~~~~ are ~~~~ ~~~~ *"THE
ESSENTIALS OF C~~~~*

D1113461

Research and Education Association
61 Ethel Road West
Piscataway, New Jersey 08854

THE ESSENTIALS®
OF COMPUTER SCIENCE I

Printed in the United States of America

Library of Congress Catalog Card Number 96-67993

International Standard Book Number 0-87891-670-9

WHAT "THE ESSENTIALS" WILL DO FOR YOU

This book is a review and study guide. It is comprehensive and it is concise.

It helps in preparing for exams, in doing homework, and remains a handy reference source at all times.

It condenses the vast amount of detail characteristic of the subject matter and summarizes the **essentials** of the field.

It will thus save hours of study and preparation time.

The book provides quick access to the important principles, concepts, theories and practices in the field.

Materials needed for exams can be reviewed in summary form – eliminating the need to read and re-read many pages of textbook and class notes. The summaries will even tend to bring detail to mind that had been previously read or noted.

This "ESSENTIALS" book has been prepared by an expert in the field, and has been carefully reviewed to assure accuracy and maximum usefulness.

Dr. Max Fogiel
Program Director

CONTENTS

Chapter 3
BOOLEAN ALGEBRA

Chapter 4
SWITCHING CIRCUITS

Chapter 5
COMPUTER ARCHITECTURE

CHAPTER 1

Fundamental Computer Concepts

There are many types of computers, from lap-tops, which use batteries and only require a minimum amount of power, to supercomputers, which are capable of billions of calculations a second and use so much power their processors need to be continuously cooled in a bath of special fluids. Computer types also range from personal computers, which are designed for a single user, to powerful mainframes, which serve hundreds of users simultaneously.

However, there are certain concepts that all computers have in common. In this chapter we will define and discuss those concepts.

1.1 Layers of a Computer System

A computer has three layers. The first layer is the hardware or the computer itself. It consists of the central processing unit, random access memory, and peripheral devices. Peripheral devices include disk drives, monitors, printers, and anything else that might be connected to a computer.

The second layer is the system software. There are three kinds of system software. The first kind is utilities, which allow users to do things like format a disk, sort a file, or set the system clock. The second kind of system software is language programs like compilers and assemblers which convert programs written by users to machine language. Since a machine language is usually unique to a type of computer, Macintosh programs won't run on IBM compatible PCs, for example. Language programs generally come with a computer.

The third and most important kind of system software is the operating system. A good definition of an operating system includes those system programs that are not utilities or language programs. A good portion of an operating system's programs or subprograms is memory resident and acts as an interface with the hardware that allows users to run other system programs and application programs.

Operating systems have what is called a kernel. The kernel is that part of the operating system which has to be very fast and efficient. Kernels are written in assembly language, which is the closest language to machine language. Kernels contain machine language instructions which perform tasks like servicing interrupts, which are interruptions of the program that is currently running. Updating the system clock every so many thousandths of a second is an example of an operating system servicing an interrupt.

In a multiprogramming environment the kernel contains a scheduler which allocates a time slice to each program that is running. If a program is waiting for input/output from a peripheral device such as a disk drive, the scheduler changes the programs status to "wait." When the disk drive's interface signals by means of an interrupt that it has the data the program requested, the operating system services the interrupt by transferring the data from the disk drive's interface to the location in memory requested by the program. It then changes the status of the program to "ready," so it will run on its next time slice. Then the operating system returns control to the program that was running so it can finish its time slice.

In a multiprogramming environment the operating system acts as a resource allocator. When a program is not able to run because it requests a file on disk that is being used by another program, a printer is not available, or the operating system is not able to allocate enough memory for the program to run, the scheduler changes the program's status to "blocked." When the resource becomes available the status is changed to "ready."

2

The operating system performs tasks that are common to every program, such as input/output, so application programs don't have to reinvent the wheel. I/O is nearly always interrupt driven. One of the reasons so many users can use a computer in a time-sharing system is because most programs spend a lot of time waiting for I/O, especially waiting for users to type on keyboards; people are very slow compared to computers.

The third layer of a computer system is the application software. Application software can be anything from a word processor to a payroll program to a scientific program running on a supercomputer. The overwhelming majority of all software run on computers is application software.

1.2 Basic Terms and Definitions

Serial Access Memory—A tape drive is a serial access memory device, which must be accessed serially by winding and unwinding a spool of magnetic tape. Tape drives are not used nearly as much as they used to be, but are still handy for backing up disk drives.

Direct Access Memory—A disk drive, which may be better thought of as semi-random access, is a direct access memory device. The movable head goes directly to the track containing the sector to be accessed, but then must wait to serially access the sector containing the actual data.

Random Access Memory—The main memory of computers is random access memory or RAM and is very fast compared to disk drives. Data may be accessed at random at any memory location. RAM is constructed from solid state electronic devices and is made up of many thousands of tiny transistors and other electronic components.

Read-Only Memory—Read-only memory is memory that can only be read; it does not have write capability. The information stored in read-only memory or ROM is made permanent during the hardware production. The advantage to ROM is that it does not lose information when the power is turned off, but still can be accessed randomly.

Track—Disk drives are electromagnetically formatted into circular tracks, with the outermost track being the largest physically and each succeeding track taking the shape of a slightly smaller circle contained in the previous track. A floppy disk might have 80 tracks while hard disks usually have thousands. A drive will usually store the same amount of data on each track regardless of its physical size.

Cylinder—A cylinder is a group of two or more concentric tracks. If a disk has one two-sided platter, then each corresponding track on the top and bottom sides of the disk is a cylinder. If a drive has four two-sided platters, each cylinder will consist of eight concentric tracks.

Sector—A disk's tracks are subdivided into sectors. Personal computer disk drives usually have sectors of 512 bytes. Each byte is made up of eight binary digits or bits.

Cluster—A cluster is made up of the corresponding sectors of the tracks that are included in the same cylinder. If a cylinder has eight tracks, then the first sector of each of the eight tracks of the cylinder represents another cluster and so on. A cluster is usually the smallest unit of file storage on a computer disk drive.

Memory—A computer's main memory or memory unit consists of RAM and contains the program or programs that are currently running, data that is being worked on by those programs, and other data that requires immediate access. The main memory is directly connected to the CPU by the "data bus" and "address lines," both of which will be discussed in Chapter 5. Interfaces between computers and peripheral devices such as monitors and disk drives also have RAMs which provide memory for the interface device, but these are distinct from the computer's main memory. When most computer scientists refer to memory or to RAM they are usually referring to the computer's main memory or memory unit.

Memory Address Space—A computer's memory is organized into words, which will be discussed in more detail in the next section. However, a word is roughly the size of one machine language instruction. Words are numbered sequentially, beginning with zero, with the numbers representing each word's address. A memory address space from decimal one hundred to decimal one thousand contains enough words for a small program or a small block of data.

Computer Languages—A computer language is a set of rules according to which a computer program is written. Computer languages are defined by their reserved words and their grammar rules.

Assembler—An assembler is a program that converts a program written in assembly language, which is the language closest to machine language that humans program in, to machine language, which the computer understands.

Compiler—A compiler is a program that converts a program written in high-level language to machine language, which the computer understands. Most compilers perform the conversion process in two steps. The first step is to convert the high-level language to assembly language or some kind of intermediate code, and the second step is to convert from the intermediate code to machine language.

Interpreter—An interpreter is a program that loads, from disk into memory, a high-level language program in its original form, rather than converting to machine language, then interprets its instructions step by step.

Program—A program is a set of instructions that tells a computer what to do. Although originally written in high-level or assembly language, most programs exist in machine language on disk. Before a program is executed, it is loaded from disk into memory by a systems program called a loader, which alters some of the machine language addresses, depending on the memory space the operating system has made available for it. The program is then executed.

Loader—A loader is a systems program that loads a machine language program from disk into memory prior to execution. Loaders are sometimes considered part of a computer's language or "translator" system, because they alter some of the machine language addresses prior to execution, and are sometimes considered part of the operating system.

Linker—A linker links together a program's modules into a single file. Programs written in high-level or assembly language often consist of separate modules in separate files, which are compiled or assembled separately into machine language. These machine language modules are linked together by a linker into a single program or "executable file," which is ready for loading and execution.

Time Sharing—Time sharing is the simultaneous use of a single computer by many users.

Multiprogramming—Multiprogramming involves the running of several programs in the computer at the same time. Each program is given a time slice of a fraction of a second.

Pseudocode—Pseudocode is a loose combination of a well-known computer language and English. Pseudocode is used by programmers in the development process of programs and in textbooks because it is more compact and much easier to understand than the code of a straight computer language which must follow strict rules. Pseudocode is used to show the logic and flow of a program or an algorithm.

Flowchart—A flowchart is a graphical representation of an algorithm or computer program.

Algorithm—An algorithm is the solution to any problem that is stated in a finite number of well-defined procedural steps. Algorithms are described with the aid of flowcharts written out in English, with each step clearly defined and numbered or shown with the use of Pseudocode. A well-defined algorithm can be easily transferred to a computer program.

Digital Systems—Digital systems used in computers are types of electronic systems that only recognize electronic signs that have a value of 0 or 1. By contrast, an analog system will allow a signal represented by a voltage to vary continuously over a specified range. Digital systems used in communications may sometimes recognize as many as eight or more signal values. A more formal definition of a digital system is a type of electronic system that only recognizes discrete values of signals.

Registers—Registers are high-speed memory devices that are part of the central processing unit and are used to manipulate data and perform arithmetic and logical operations.

Central Processing Unit (CPU)—The central processing unit is made up of registers, the arithmetic logic unit, and the control unit. The central processing unit reads and writes from memory, and executes machine language instructions. The CPU is sometimes called the brains of the computer.

BIOS—BIOS stands for Basic Input Output System. The BIOS contains those machine language instructions that are necessary to load the operating system from disk into memory. The BIOS contains the "boot-strap" program which is used to "boot-up" the computer when the power is turned on. The BIOS continues to be part of the operating system while the computer is running. The BIOS is stored in ROM so it will not be erased when the power is turned off.

Distributed Processing System—A type of computer system or computer network that distributes control, data, and processing capability rather than concentrating control and processing in one processing unit or one main computer. A distributed processing system can be one computer with many processors and distributed control and memory or it can be a computer network with distributed control, data, and processing power. Usually the term "distributer processing system" refers to a type of computer network.

Data Processing—The best way to think of data processing is as the service provided by the data processing departments of institutions such as corporations, universities, and city governments. Most universities offer a business information systems major or the equivalent. Data processing departments recruit business information systems majors to work as systems analysts and programmers who specialize in putting together hardware and software systems already available on the market with in-house produced software to improve the quality of the data processing of the institution they serve. Core computer science majors, on the other hand, are trained in the development of systems software *before* a new computer appears on the market, or in the development of programs for *scientific* or *engineering* applications. The still relatively new field of software engineering, which was created to bring engineering discipline to software development, has resulted in core computer science majors increasingly ending up in data processing environments as software engineers. A formal definition of data processing is the collecting, processing, and distributing of facts to achieve a desired result.

1.3 Units of Storage

The most basic unit of storage is the bit or binary digit. A bit can be a 0 or a 1, corresponding to on or off.

A byte is a group of 8 bits.

A word is either 1, 2, 4, or 8 bytes, depending on the size of the registers, or high-speed memory devices, in the computers central processing unit. A word represents how much data is transferred to or from the central processing unit to the RAM with each memory access.

A kilobyte is 2^{10} or 1,024 bytes. This number is the closest power of two to one thousand. The size of a file is often described in terms of kilobytes.

A megabyte is 2^{20} or 1,046,516 bytes. This number is the closest power of two to one million. Computer memory and many disk drives are referred to in terms of megabytes.

A gigabyte is 2^{30} of 1,073,741,824 bytes. This number is the closest power of two to one billion. The newest large hard drives are referred to in terms of gigabytes.

1.4 Computer Languages

There are many computer languages, in fact hundreds. However, we will try to highlight the more important ones.

BASIC—BASIC is an interpretive language, which means it is run by an interpreter rather than compiled. It is good for a beginner to learn.

Pascal—Pascal was named for the French mathematician of that name. It was derived from the now antique language of ALGOL and is one of the languages which is closest to English. It is often used for teaching, because it tends to lead students into proper programming techniques.

ADA—ADA was named after the first programmer, who was the wife of an English nobleman and who tried to program Charles Babbage's analytical engine in the early 1800s. Some of the major constructs of today's programs, such as loops and branches, were used in her programs. ADA was developed by the defense department with the idea that all of their programs could be written in ADA. An ADA program is completely portable, which means it will run on any computer. ADA is very similar to Pascal.

C—C language is also similar to Pascal but much more cryptic. It got the name C because it was derived from Beta language (Beta being the Greek letter for "B") which was developed for the Beta test of an earlier version of the Unix operating system. C language was used to write the first working version of Unix, developed at Bell Laboratories. C language has become the most commonly used language for personal computer application programs.

C++—C++ is a popular version of C language that includes object oriented programming.

LISP—LISP, an acronym for, List processing language, was developed for artificial intelligence applications and is extensively used for artificial intelligence research in the United States.

Prolog—Prolog is used for artificial intelligence research in Japan.

FORTRAN—FORTRAN, which stands for formula translation, was the first high-level language developed in 1957 and is still used extensively for scientific applications. Supercomputers are programmed in FORTRAN for research applications such as flight simulation.

COBOL—COBOL, an acronym for COmmon Business Oriented Language, is also one of the first computer languages and is used extensively for business applications.

Assembly—Assembly language is unique to each computer system or microprocessor series, but the same constructs run through all versions of assembly language. Assembly language is the closest language to machine language programmed by humans. Assembly language programming requires extensive knowledge of the computer's architecture, the subject of Chapter 5.

FORTH—Fourth generation language is half-way between assembly and high-level languages. FORTH is both an operating system and a language. FORTH is an attempt to force the programmer to emphasize the flow of data and to write programs which are as close as possible to English.

Smalltalk—Smalltalk emphasizes object oriented programming, which is a growing computer science design philosophy.

CHAPTER 2

Number Representations

Digital computer systems are built from a large number of digital electronic circuits. The output of a digital electronic circuit is called a bit, a number which may have only two values, 0 and 1. In the binary number system, each bit represents a binary digit, and binary numbers are made up of one or more bits.

Digital circuits use a range of voltages to define logic 0 and logic 1. In TTL circuits (transistor-transistor logic is one of the logic families used in computers) any voltage between 0 and 0.8 V is a 0 and any voltage from +2 to +5 is a 1. By restricting the value of the output to one of two values, any imprecision that might be the result of aging of the circuit or other minor factors can be avoided. For example, a voltage of 3.51 and a voltage of 3.52 are both interpreted as logic 1. Thus, minor imprecisions in the circuit become immaterial. The need for precision has resulted in the use of digital electronic circuits in computers, and the only number system that digital circuits can work with is the binary number system.

2.1 Number Bases and Notation

Humans who use computers sometimes have reason to work with numbers the way computers store or use numbers, in binary form. Sometimes these numbers are more conveniently represented in octal form, base 8, or hexadecimal form, base 16. Notice that both 8 and 16 are powers of 2.

11

The way numbers are represented, to avoid confusion about their bases, is with a subscript. For example, 375_{10} represents the number 375 of base 10. The value of a number depends upon the magnitude of its digits and on their position. The value of a number is the sum of the least significant digit times the base raised to the 0 power, plus the next significant digit times the base raised to the first power, and so on, up to the most significant digit, as shown in Figure 2.1.

	1011_2					367_8		
	1	×	2^0	1				
+	1	×	2^1	2	+	7	×	8^0	7
+	0	×	2^2	0	+	6	×	8^1	48
+	1	×	2^3	8	+	3	×	8^2	192
				11_{10}					247_{10}

$$1011_2$$

$$1 \times 2^0 \quad 1$$
$$+ \ 1 \times 2^1 \quad 2$$
$$+ \ 0 \times 2^2 \quad 0$$
$$+ \ 1 \times 2^3 \quad 8$$
$$\overline{11_{10}}$$

$$367_8$$

$$+ \ 7 \times 8^0 \quad 7$$
$$+ \ 6 \times 8^1 \quad 48$$
$$+ \ 3 \times 8^2 \quad 192$$
$$\overline{247_{10}}$$

$$3168_{10}$$

$$8 \times 10^0 \quad 8$$
$$+ \ 6 \times 10^1 \quad 60$$
$$+ \ 1 \times 10^2 \quad 100$$
$$+ \ 3 \times 10^3 \quad 3000$$
$$\overline{3168_{10}}$$

$$B64_{16}$$

$$+ \ 4 \times 16^0 \quad 4$$
$$+ \ 6 \times 16^1 \quad 96$$
$$+ \ B \times 16^3 \quad 2816$$
$$\overline{2916_{16}}$$

Fig 2.1 Decimal Values of Numbers of Base 2, 8, 10, 16

In hexadecimal, or base 16, we use the letters A through F to represent the decimal equivalent of 10 through 15. For example, the B in B64 shown in Figure 2.1 represents the decimal equivalent of 11.

When working with number bases commonly used by computer scientists, the equivalents shown in Table 2.1 are helpful, and can, with practice, be committed to memory.

Binary (2)	Octal (8)	Decimal (10)	Hexadecimal (16)
000	0	0	0
001	1	1	1
010	2	2	2
011	3	3	3
100	4	4	4
101	5	5	5
110	6	6	6
111	7	7	7
1000	10	8	8
1001	11	9	9
1010	12	10	A
1011	13	11	B
1100	14	12	C
1101	15	13	D
1110	16	14	E
1111	17	15	F

Table 2.1 Equivalents of Binary, Octal, Decimal, and Hexadecimal

We will show, in the following sections, how to convert any number of base 2, 8, 10, and 16 to its equivalent in the other three bases, then we will show how computers perform binary arithmetic operations.

2.2 Conversions from Base 10 to Other Bases

2.2.1 To Base 2

To convert an integer of base 10 to an integer of base 2, divide repeatedly by the base and save the remainder.

EXAMPLE

Convert 17_{10} to base 2.

2	17	
	8	1
	4	0
	2	0
	1	0
	0	1

$= 10,001_2$

To convert a fraction of base 10 to a fraction of base 2, multiply repeatedly by the base and save the integer part.

EXAMPLE

Convert $.75_{10}$ to base 2.

$$
\begin{array}{r}
.75 \\
\times 2 \\
\hline
\underline{1}.50 \quad 1 \\
2 \\
\hline
\underline{1}.00 \quad 1 \\
2 \\
\hline
\underline{0}.00 \quad 0
\end{array}
$$

$= .110_2$

To convert a mixed number of base 10 to a mixed number of base 2, divide the integer part repeatedly by the new base, multiply the fraction part by the new base, and add the results.

14

EXAMPLE

Convert 9.32_{10} to base 2, up to four places after decimal point.

```
2 | 9  |                              .32
   |----+---                          ×2
   | 4  | 1                        --------
   |----+---                        0.64
   | 2  | 0                          ×2
   |----+---                        --------
   | 1  | 0                        1.28
   |----+---                          ×2
   | 0  | 1   =   1001₂            --------
                                    056
              1001.0000               ×2
            +    .0101              --------
              ---------            1.12   =   .0101₂
              1001.0101₂
```

2.2.2 To Base 8

To convert an integer of base 10 to an integer of base 8, divide repeatedly by the base and save the remainder.

EXAMPLE

Convert 1321_{10} to base 8.

```
8 | 1321  |
  |--------+---
  |  165   | 1
  |--------+---
  |   20   | 5
  |--------+---
  |    2   | 4
  |--------+---
  |    0   | 2   =   2451₈
```

To convert a fraction of base 8 to a fraction of base 10, multiply repeatedly by the base and save the integer part.

EXAMPLE

Convert $.390625_{10}$ to base 8.

$$.390625$$
$$\underline{\times \quad 8}$$
$$\underline{3}.125000$$
$$\underline{\times \quad 8}$$
$$\underline{1}.000000$$
$$\underline{\times \quad 8}$$
$$0.000000 \quad = \quad .31_8$$

To convert a mixed number from base 10 to a mixed number of base 8, divide the integer part repeatedly by the new base, multiply the fraction part repeatedly by the new base, and add the results.

EXAMPLE

Convert 17.75_{10} to base 8.

```
8 |  17  |                    .75
   |_____|                   ×8
   |  2   | 1                _____
   |_____|                  6.00
   |  0   | 2  =  21₈          8
   |_____|                 _____
                            0.00  =  .60₈
```

$$21.00$$
$$\underline{+ \; .60}$$
$$21.60_8$$

2.2.3 To Base 16

To convert a number of base 10 to a number of base 16, first convert to base 2, then put the binary number into quartets (groups of four bits), and use Table 2.1 to convert to hexadecimal.

EXAMPLE

Convert 217.25_{10} to base 16.

```
2 | 217 |                              .25
  ─────                              ×2
    108 | 1                        ──────
  ─────                             0.50
     54 | 0                          ×2
  ─────                            ──────
     27 | 0                         1.00
  ─────                              ×2
     13 | 1                        ──────
  ─────                             0.00   =   .010₂
      6 | 1
  ─────
      3 | 0
  ─────
      1 | 1
  ─────
      0 | 1   =   11011001₂
```

$$11011001.000$$
$$\underline{+\ .010}$$
$$11011001.010_2$$

Group by four bits and obtain hexadecimal equivalents from Table 2.1.

$$1\ 1\ 0\ 1 \quad 1\ 0\ 0\ 1 \quad \cdot \quad 0\ 1\ 0\ 0$$

$$\lfloor \quad D \quad \rfloor \quad \lfloor \quad 9 \quad \rfloor \cdot \lfloor \quad 4 \quad \rfloor$$

$$217.25_{10} = D9.4_{16}$$

2.3 Conversions from Other Bases to Base 10

To convert from other bases to base 10, multiply each digit times the old base raised to the power that is determined by counting how many places the digit is to the right or left of the binary, octal, or hexadecimal point (to the left is positive and to the right is negative, as shown in the example below). Then add the results of the multiplication.

EXAMPLE

   a. Convert 11101.101_2 to base 10.

b. Convert 547_8 to base 10.

c. Convert $4B3.C_{16}$ to base 10.

  a. 11101.101_2

$$(1 \times 2^4) + (1 \times 2^3) + (1 \times 2^2) + (0 \times 2^1) + (1 \times 2^0)$$
$$+ (1 \times 2^{-1}) + (0 \times 2^{-2}) + (1 \times 2^{-3})$$

$$= (1 \times 16) + (1 \times 8) + (1 \times 4) + (0 \times 2) + (1 \times 1)$$
$$+ (1 \times .5) + (0 \times .25) + (1 \times .125)$$

$$= 29.625_{10}$$

  b. 547_8

$$(5 \times 8^2) + (4 \times 8^1) + (7 \times 8^0) =$$

$$(5 \times 64) + (4 \times 8) + (7 \times 1) = 359_{10}$$

  c. $4B3.C_{16}$

$$= (4 \times 16^2) + (B \times 16^1) + (3 \times 16^0) + (C \times 16^{-1})$$

$$= (4 \times 256) + (11 \times 16) + (3 \times 1)(12 \times .0625)$$

$$= 1203.0625_{10}$$

2.4 Conversion Among Bases 2, 8, and 16

2.4.1 Conversion from Base 2 to Base 8 and Base 16

To convert from base 2 to base 8 or base 16, group the binary number into triads or quartets and use Table 2.1 to find the octal or hexadecimal equivalents for each digit.

EXAMPLE

  a. Convert 111011.01_2 to base 8.

  b. Convert 11010110111_2 to base 16.

a. 111011.01_2

Group into triads and find octal equivalents in Table 2.1.

$$\underline{|111|011|} \cdot \underline{|010|}$$
$$\quad 7 \quad\quad 3 \quad\quad\quad 2$$

$$= 73.2_8$$

b. 11010110111_2

Group into quartets and find hexadecimal equivalents in Table 2.1.

$$\underline{|0110|1011|0111|}$$
$$\quad 6 \quad\quad B \quad\quad 7$$

$$= 6B7_{16}$$

2.4.2 Conversion from Base 8 and Base 16 to Base 2

To convert from base 8 or base 16 to base 2, look up the binary equivalent of each octal or hexadecimal digit in Table 2.1.

EXAMPLE

a. Convert $3B5_{16}$ to base 2.

b. Convert 243.7_8 to base 2.

a. $3B5_{16}$

Look up the binary equivalent in Table 2.1 for each hexadecimal digit.

$$\quad 3 \quad\quad B \quad\quad\quad 5$$
$$\underline{|0011|1011|0101|}$$

$$= 1110110101_2$$

b. 243.7_8

Look up the binary equivalent in Table 2.1 for each octal digit.

19

$$\begin{array}{cccc} 2 & 4 & 3 & \cdot \quad 7 \\ \lfloor 010 \rfloor\, 100 \rfloor\, 011 \rfloor & \cdot \lfloor 111 \rfloor \end{array}$$

$$= 10100011.111_2$$

2.4.3 Conversion Between Base 8 and Base 16

To convert between base 8 and base 16, first convert to binary, then regroup binary number into triads or quartets.

EXAMPLE

a. Convert 7653_8 to base 16.

b. Convert $D7.5_{16}$ to base 8.

a. 7653_8

Obtain binary triad from Table 2.1, from memory, or by mentally deriving it, for each octal digit.

$$\begin{array}{cccc} 7 & 6 & 5 & 3 \\ \lfloor 111 \mid 110 \mid 101 \mid 011 \rfloor \end{array}$$

Regroup into quartets and write hexadecimal equivalent.

$$\begin{array}{ccc} \lfloor 1111 \mid 1010 \mid 1011 \rfloor \\ F & A & B \end{array}$$

$$= FAB_{16}$$

b. $D7.5_{16}$

Write binary quartets.

$$\begin{array}{ccc} D & 7 & \cdot \quad 5 \\ \lfloor 1101 \mid 0111 \rfloor & \cdot \lfloor 0101 \rfloor \end{array}$$

Regroup into triads and write octal equivalents.

$$\begin{array}{cccccc} \lfloor 011 \mid 010 \mid 111 \rfloor & \cdot \lfloor 010 \mid 100 \rfloor \\ 3 & 2 & 7 & \cdot & 2 & 4 \end{array}$$

$$= 327.24_8$$

20

2.5 Mathematical Operations Using Binary Numbers

2.5.1 Addition Using Binary Numbers

Binary addition is like decimal addition except there is a carry whenever the sum of a column is more than one rather than more than nine. Computers don't add more than two numbers at a time, so we will only show the addition of two numbers.

EXAMPLE

Add 101011_2 to 100111_2

$$
\begin{array}{r}
101011 \\
+100111 \\
\hline
1010010_2
\end{array}
$$

2.5.2 Subtraction Using Binary Numbers

There are two forms of subtraction performed by computers. The first is similar to decimal subtraction except there is a borrow whenever 1 is subtracted from 0.

EXAMPLE

Subtract 101001_2 from 110011_2.

$$
\begin{array}{ll}
\text{Column} & 654321 \\
\hline
& 110011 \\
& 101001 \\
\hline
& 001010_2
\end{array}
$$

1. Column 1 $1 - 1 = 0$
2. Column 2 $1 - 0 = 1$
3. Column 3 $0 - 0 = 0$
4. Column 4 $0 - 1 = 1$ The 1 in column 5 is changed to a 0 due to a borrow generated in column 4.

21

5. Column 5   This is now $0 - 0 = 0$

6. Column 6 $1 - 1 = 0$

The first form of subtraction is shown in this example. This assumes that the arithmetic logic unit of a computer has a full subtractor, which it may not.

Computers also perform subtraction by forming what is called the two's complement of the subtrahend and then adding it to the minuend. The two's complement is formed by first complementing each bit of a binary number, to form the one's complement, and then adding 1, to form the two's complement of the subtrahend. In this example first complement then add 1:

$$
\begin{array}{ll}
00101001 & \\
11010110 & - \quad \text{one's complement} \\
\underline{1} & - \quad \text{add one} \\
11010111_2 & - \quad \text{two's complement}
\end{array}
$$

We now have the negative of the subtrahend for this example.

Computers store and perform arithmetic operations on integers of groups of 8 bits, or bytes, called words. A word is usually 2 or more bytes, although for a simple computer a word might be one byte. For a signed integer, the most significant bit is the sign bit. For a 1 byte integer, bit 7 is the sign bit, with bits 0–6 representing the magnitude. Notice that when we formed the two's complement above, bit 7 was a 1, indicating a negative integer. For signed integers a most significant bit of 0 indicates a positive integer.

The reason a lot of computers use two's complement arithmetic is because it is convenient to represent the sign of an integer with the most significant bit.

The next example shows subtraction performed by adding the two's complement; the values of the minuend and subtrahend are the same as in the previous example except they have been extended to a full byte by placing 0s in bit 6 and bit 7.

EXAMPLE

Subtract 00101001_2 from 00110011_2

First form the two's complement of the subtrahend by complementing and adding 1.

$$
\begin{array}{ll}
00101001 & \\
11010110 & \text{one's complement} \\
\underline{+1} & \\
11010111_2 & \text{two's complement}
\end{array}
$$

Now add to the minuend.

$$
\begin{array}{l}
00110011 \\
\underline{+11010111} \\
00001010_2
\end{array}
$$

The result is the same as in the previous example.

2.5.3   Multiplication of a Binary Number

Computers perform multiplication by shifting and adding. Integers to be multiplied are stored in registers of one word length. If, for example, a computer had a word length of 2 bytes (16 bits) and the result of a multiplication would have been a 17 bit binary number, the accumulator, the register which contains the results of arithmetic operations, would overflow, resulting in an error condition. This doesn't mean that computers can never perform arithmetic operations when the result is more than one word length, but to do so they have to be programmed to save partial products, and to store the final result in adjacent words.

For our example of multiplication we will assume a word length of 1 byte and a multiplier and multiplicand of four significant binary digits, so there is no chance of an overflow. Binary multiplication is carried out by computers by sequences of shifting and adding, or by shifts alone. The number and then the order of each is determined by the multiplier digits. The multiplier is examined from right to left, bit by bit. If the bit is 1, addition and shifting is carried out, if the bit is 0, only shifting is carried out, as shown in the following example.

23

EXAMPLE

Multiply 01011_2 times 01101_2.

01101	Multiplicand
01011	Multiplier
00001101	Enter right bit times multiplicand
00011010	Next bit times multiplicand, shift
00100111	Add
00110100	Shift alone, bit 2 of multiplier is 0
00100111	No addition
01101000	Next bit times multiplicand, shift
10001111_2	Add to get result

Multiplication of reals, called "floating point multiplication" with regard to computer operations, is similar to multiplication of decimal numbers represented in scientific notation, except the mantissa is entirely to the right of the binary point. The sign is represented by a binary digit just to the left of the binary point, and the exponent is a power of two, with the leftmost bit the sign bit. For example:

Mantissa	**Exponent**
1.11010_2	0101_2

The above binary real would represent a negative (because the sign bit is 1) binary fraction whose decimal equivalent is $-.625$ times 2^5 which equals -20.

Although floating point multiplication is more complicated than integer multiplication, it is carried out by multiplying the mantissas, in a way similar to integer multiplication, and then adding the exponents.

2.5.4 Division of Binary Numbers

Computers perform fixed point division by shifting and subtracting. If the subtraction would result in a negative, the subtraction is inhibited. The following example shows integer binary division.

24

EXAMPLE

Divide 00100000_2 by 00000110_2.

00100000	Dividend
11101000	Two complement of divisor
00001000	Add to find partial remainder
11110100	Shift and form two's complement
	Result would be negative, inhibited

answer = 000010002

Computers perform floating division by dividing the mantissa of the divisor into the mantissa of the dividend and then subtracting the exponents.

CHAPTER 3

Boolean Algebra

The basic mathematics needed for the design of switching systems is Boolean Algebra. Boolean Algebra is applied extensively in other areas such as set theory and mathematical logic, but we will focus on its application to switching systems.

3.1 Basic Operations

The basic operations are AND, OR, and inverse.

The AND operation can be defined as follows:

$$\emptyset \cdot \emptyset = \emptyset, \emptyset \cdot 1 = \emptyset, 1 \cdot \emptyset = \emptyset, 1 \cdot 1 = 1$$

and can be represented by the following table:

A	B	A · B
0	0	0
0	1	0
1	0	0
1	1	1

Table 3.1

The OR operation can be defined as follows:

$$0 + 0 = 0, 0 + 1 = 1, 1 + 0 = 1, 1 + 1 = 1$$

and can be represented by the following table:

A	B	$A + B$
0	0	0
0	1	0
1	0	0
1	1	1

Table 3.2

The inverse (or complement) can be defined as follows:

$$1' = 0 \quad 0 = 1'$$

if $A = 1$ then $A' = 0$, and if $A = 0$ then $A' = 1$.

3.2 Basic Laws of Boolean Algebra

The basic laws of Boolean Algebra are:

1A: $A + A = A$ [Idempotent law for +]
1B: $A \cdot A = A$ [Idempotent law for ·]
2A: $A + B = B + A$ [Commutative law for +]
2B: $A \cdot B = B \cdot A$ [Commutative law for ·]
3A: $A + (B + C) = (A + B) + C$ [Associative law for +]
3B: $A \cdot (B \cdot C) = (A \cdot B) \cdot C$ [Associative law for ·]
4A: $A \cdot (B + C) = (A \cdot B) + (A \cdot C)$
        [Distributive law for · over +]
4B: $A + (B \cdot C) = (A + B) \cdot (A + C)$
        [Distributive law for + over ·]
5A: $A + 1 = 1$ (Law of Union)
5B: $A \cdot 0 = 0$ (Law of Intersection)
6A: $A \cdot 1 = A$ [1 is the identity element for ·]
6B: $A + 0 = A$ [0 is the identity element for +]

The laws of ~:

7:     $(A')' = A$ [Double Negative Law or Involution Law]
8A: $A + A' = 1$
8B: $A \cdot \sim A = 0$ [Law of Complement]
9A: $(A + B)' = A' \cdot B'$ [DeMorgan's Law]
9B: $(A \cdot B)' = A' + B'$ [DeMorgan's Law]
10:     $1' = 0$ and $0' = 1$

27

Any system obeying these laws with the basic operations $(+, \cdot)$ is a Boolean Algebra. All of these laws can be shown to be true by setting up its truth table. Truth tables will be discussed in the next section.

Actually only eight properties need to be satisfied, since the other ten follow immediately. In fact, it can be shown by applying DeMorgan's Laws that a Boolean Algebra needs only one of the two operators $(+, \cdot)$ together with the inverse function to be functionally complete.

The "$\cdot$" operator is often not shown and we will usually write "AB" instead of $A \cdot B$. Here is an additional theorem that may be useful:

Law of Absorption: $A(A + B) = A$
$$A + AB = A$$

EXAMPLE

Simplify the following expressions according to the commutative law.

(a) $AB' + B'A + CDE + C'DE + EC'D$

(b) $AB + AC + BA$

(c) $(LMN)(AB)(CDE)(MNL)$

(d) $F(K + R) + SV + WX' + VS + X'W + (R + K)F$

The commutative law states that:

$$AB = BA; A + B = B + A$$

Thus, when logic symbols are ANDed or ORed, the order in which they are written does not affect their value.

(a) Notice that AB' and $B'A$ and $C'DE$ and $EC'D$ are equal to each other—only their order is changed. The idempotent law states that $A + A = A$ and $AA = A$. Thus, any term ANDed or ORed with itself will be equal to itself. The equation is rewritten as

$$AB' + CDE + C'DE$$

28

(b) Similarly, AB and BA are combined to form AB. Therefore, we get

$$AB + AC$$

(c) Remember that the commutative and indempotent laws are also true for the AND operation. Thus, LMN and MNL combine to form LMN

$$(LMN)\,(AB)\,(CDE)$$

(d) In this case: $F(K + R) = (R + K)\,F$, $SV = VS$, and $WX' = X'W$, again by the commutative law. Therefore, our result is

$$F\,(K + R) + SV + WX'$$

EXAMPLE

Apply DeMorgan's theorem to the following equations:

(a) $F = (V + A + L)'$

(b) $F = A' + B' + C' + D'$

DeMorgan's theorem states that a logical expression can be complemented by complementing all its variables and exchanging AND ($\cdot$) operations with OR (+) operations. For example, the complement of

$$F = AB$$

is

$$F' - A' + B'$$

Another expression for F is found by complementing F'.

$$F = (F')' = (A' + B')'$$

thus

$$(A' + B')' = AB$$

(a) Complementing variables V, A, L, and changing "+" to "$\cdot$", we get

$$F' = (V' \cdot A' \cdot L')' \text{ (Note } AB = A \cdot B)$$

29

Complement the entire expression to find F,

$$F = (F')' = [(V'A'L')] = V'A'L'$$

(b) Again, complementing A, B, C, and D and changing "+" to "." we get

$$F' = ABCD$$

$$F = (F') = (ABCD)'$$

EXAMPLE

Simplify the following expressions

(a) $A = TUV + XY + Y$

(b) $A = F(E + F + G)$

We need the law of absorption to simplify these expressions:

Law of Absorption: $A(A + B) = A$

$A + AB = A$

(a) $A = TUV + XY + Y$

Use the law of absorption on XY and Y

$A = TUV + Y$

(b) $A = F(E + F + G)$

Use the distributive law

$$A = FE + FF + FG$$

Use the idempotent law on FF

$$A = FE + F + FG$$

Use the law of absorption

$$A = F$$

30

3.3 Logic Status

There is a one-to-one correspondence between Boolean Algebra and switching circuits. Figure 3.1 and Figure 3.2 show the switching circuits analogous to the AND operation and the OR operation, respectively.

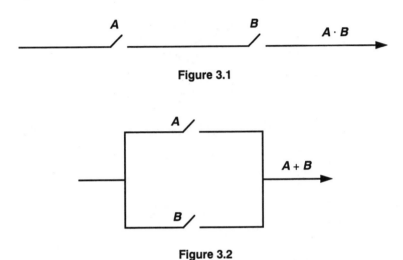

Figure 3.1

Figure 3.2

Figures 3.3 and 3.4 show the logic gate representation for the AND and OR operations. The symbolic representation for the inversion function, referred to as an "inverter," is shown in Figure 3.5.

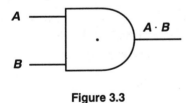

Figure 3.3

31

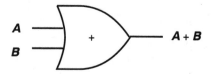

Figure 3.4

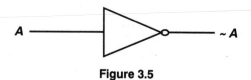

Figure 3.5

The gate representation for the expression $(A + C + D) \cdot A \cdot B'$ is:

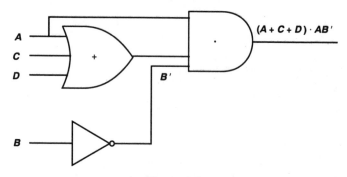

Figure 3.6

For the next two logic gates we need to introduce two more operators. The ↑ operator is called the Schaffer stroke function and its associated gate is the NAND (for NOT-AND) and it can be defined as:

$$A \uparrow B = (A \cdot B)'$$

The ↓ operator's associated gate is the NOR (for NOT-OR) and can be defined as:

$$A \downarrow B = (A + B)'$$

32

Figures 3.7 and 3.8 show the logic gate representation of the NAND and NOR gates, respectively.

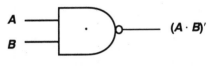

$(A \cdot B)'$

Figure 3.7

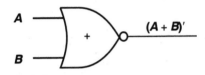

$(A + B)'$

Figure 3.8

For the next logic gates we will need to introduce the ⊕ operator. The ⊕ operator's associated gate is the EXCLUSIVE-OR. EXCLUSIVE-OR differs from the previously defined OR in that $A \oplus B = 1$, if A is 1 and B is 0 or A is 0 and B is 1, and it can be defined as:

$$A \oplus B = A' B + AB'$$

For the last logic gate we will introduce the ≡ operator. The ≡ operator's associated gate is the EQUIVALENCE. $A \equiv B = 1$ if $A = B$, then the EQUIVALENCE is the complement of EXCLUSIVE-OR, and we can write

$$A \equiv B = (A \oplus B)' = AB + A'B'$$

Figure 3.9 shows the logic gate representation of the EQUIVALENCE.

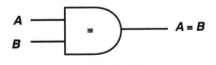

$A \equiv B$

Figure 3.9

33

3.4 Truth Tables

A truth table specifies the value of a Boolean expression for every possible combination of values in an expression.

EXAMPLE

The truth table for the Boolean expression $(A + B) \cdot C$ is

A	B	C	$(A + B) \cdot C$
0	0	0	0
0	0	1	0
0	1	0	0
0	1	1	1
1	0	0	0
1	0	1	1
1	1	0	0
1	1	1	1

Table 3.3

The name "truth table" comes from a similar table used in mathematical logic to show the truth or falsity of each statement.

Sometimes truth tables are used to break down a Boolean expression into smaller parts and thus are used as a tool for evaluating the whole expression.

EXAMPLE

The truth table for the Boolean expression $AB' \cdot (A + B)$ is

A	B	B'	AB'	$A + B$	$AB' \cdot (A + B)$
0	0	1	0	0	0
0	1	0	0	1	0
1	0	1	1	1	1
1	1	0	0	1	0

Table 3.4

We can use truth tables to specify the output of switching circuits.

EXAMPLE

Specify the output of the gate representation of the Boolean expression $A'B + C$ using a truth table.

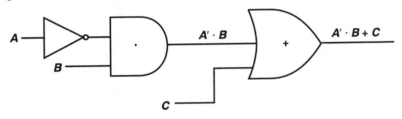

Figure 3.10

A	B	C	A'	$A'B$	$A'B + C$
0	0	0	1	0	0
0	0	1	1	0	1
0	1	0	1	1	1
0	1	1	1	1	1
1	0	0	0	0	0
1	0	1	0	0	1
1	1	0	0	0	0
1	1	1	0	0	1

Table 3.5

3.5   Karnaugh Maps

Consider this equation:

$$f = AB'C' + A'BC + AB'C \qquad (3.5.1)$$

Each of the terms in equation (3.5.1) is referred to as a minterm. In Boolean Algebra, a minterm is the product of n literals (a literal is a variable or a complement) in which each variable appears once in true or complemented form. Minterms are often abbreviated m_0, m, etc. Table 3.6 lists all the minterms for the three variables, A, B, C.

35

A function f that is written as a sum of minterms is referred to as a minterm expansion. Equation (3.5.1) can be rewritten as

$$f(A, B, C) = m_3 + m_4 + m_5 \qquad (3.5.2)$$

or as
$$f(A, B, C) = \Sigma m\,(3, 4, 5) \qquad (3.5.2a)$$

Consider this equation:

$$f = (A' + B + C)\,(A + B' + C')\,(A' + B + C') \qquad (3.5.3)$$

Each of the terms in equation (3.5.3) is referred to as a maxterm. A maxterm is the sum of n literals in which each variable appears once in true or complemented form. Maxterms are often abbreviated M_0, M_1, etc. Table 3.6 lists all the maxterms for the three variables A, B, C.

A function f that is written as a product of maxterms is referred to as a maxterms expansion. Equation (3.5.3) can be rewritten as

$$f(A, B, C) = M_2\,M_3\,M_4 = TTM\,(2, 3, 4) \qquad (3.5.4)$$

Row no.	ABC	Minterms	Maxterms
0	0 0 0	$A'B'C' = m_0$	$A + B + C\ \ = M_0$
1	0 0 1	$A'B'C = m_1$	$A + B + C' = M_1$
2	0 1 0	$A'BC' = m_2$	$A + B' + C\ = M_2$
3	0 1 1	$A'BC = m_3$	$A + B' + C' = M_3$
4	1 0 0	$AB'C' = m_4$	$A' + B + C\ = M_4$
5	1 0 1	$AB'C = m_5$	$A' + B + C' = M_5$
6	1 1 0	$ABC' = m_6$	$A' + B + C\ = M_6$
7	1 1 1	$ABC = m_7$	$A' + B' + C' = M_7$

Table 3.6 Minterms and Maxterms for Three Variables

Karnaugh maps (which are generally used for circuit minimization which is discussed in the next section), are similar to truth tables in that they specify the value of the function for every combination of the function's interdependent variable. We show how to specify a Karnaugh map for minterm and maxterm expansions of two, three, and four variables by means of examples. Note—different notations are used to write the function but the functions in all three examples are m or M expanses.

36

EXAMPLE

Specify the Karnaugh map for

$$f(A, B) = AB + AB'$$

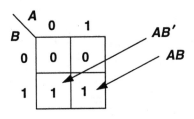

Figure 3.11

EXAMPLE

Specify the Karnaugh map for

$$f(A, B, C) = M_3 + M_4 + M_5$$

The rows are labeled in sequence 00, 01, 11, 01 so that the values in adjacent rows differ in only one variable. We place a small decimal number corresponding to each possible minterm in the corner of each square and mark the squares corresponding to the minterms in the expansion with a 1 and the remaining with a 0.

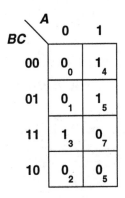

Figure 3.12

37

EXAMPLE

Specify the Karnaugh map for

$$f = \Pi M \,(3, 5, 7, 12, 13)$$

We label the rows and columns of each square so that the values in adjacent squares differ by only one variable. We place a 0 in the squares corresponding to each maxterm in the expansion and 1s in the remaining squares.

BC \ AB	00	01	11	10
00	0_0	1_4	0_{12}	1_8
01	1_1	0_5	0_{13}	1_9
11	0_3	0_7	1_{15}	1_{11}
10	1_2	1_6	1_{14}	1_{10}

Figure 3.13

Boolean expressions which are not in minterm or maxterm expansion form can also be specified by Karnaugh maps.

EXAMPLE

Specify the Karnaugh map for

$$f(A, B, C) = A' B' C + A' B + A$$

The $A' B' C$ term is specified by marking the square labeled 001 with a 1. The $A' B$ term is specified by marking squares labeled 011 and 010 with 1s because we don't know if C is high or low. The A term is specified by marking the squares labeled 100, 101, 111, and 110 with 1s because we don't know if B or C is high or low. The remaining square is marked with a 0.

Boolean expressions that are are not in minterm or maxterm form can be converted to a minterm or maxterm expansion by rather straight-forward algebraic manipulation. However, it is easier to simply use a Karnaugh map.

3.6 Circuit Minimization

A switching network which corresponds to a switching function can often be greatly reduced in complexity by applying the laws of Boolean Algebra, as seen in the following example.

EXAMPLE

Draw an equivalent network which will give the same output function as in Figure 3.14, using the minimum amount of gates.

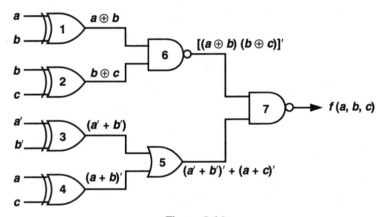

Figure 3.14

The output function $f(a, b, c)$ is:

$$f(a, b, c) = \left[[(a \oplus b) \cdot (b \oplus c)]' \cdot [(a' + b') + (a + c)']\right]'$$

By the use of Boolean Algebra theorems, this function can be reduced as follows:

Apply DeMorgan's Law and Involution Law

$$f(a, b, c) = [(a \oplus b) \cdot (b \oplus c)] + [(a' + b')' \cdot (a + c)']'$$

Use definition of exclusive OR function

$$f(a, b, c) = (ab' + a'b) \cdot (bc' + b'c) + (a' + b') \cdot (a + c)$$

Apply Distributive Law and Law of Complement

$$f(a, b, c) = 0 + ab'c + 0 + b'a + b'c + a'c$$

Apply Indentity Laws to 0 terms and Law of Absorption to $ab'c$ and $b'c$ terms

$$f(a, b, c) = ab'c + a'bc' + a'c + ab'$$

Apply DeMorgan's Law to $ab'c$ and $a'c$ terms

$$f(a, b, c) = b'c + a'bc' + a'c + ab'$$

Apply DeMorgan's Law to $a'bc'$ and $a'c$ terms

$$f(a, b, c) = b'c + a'b + a'c + ab'$$

Apply DeMorgan's Law

$$f(a, b, c) = b'c + a'b + ab'$$

Use definition of EXCLUSIVE-OR

$$f(a, b, c) = b'c + a \oplus b$$

The final function can now be translated into a switching network by the use of AND, OR, and EXCLUSIVE-OR gates as shown in Figure 3.15.

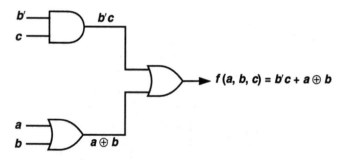

Figure 3.15

A switching function can generally be simplified by using algebraic techniques, but the procedures are difficult to apply in a systematic way and it is hard to tell when a minimum solution has been reached. These difficulties are overcome by using Karnaugh maps for circuit minimization.

Before the next example is presented, six concepts must be understood.

1. 1s in Karnaugh maps specified by minterm expansions (0s in the case of maxterm expansions) can be grouped together in groups of 1, 2, 4, 8, etc. if they are in adjacent squares (see Figure 3.16).

2. Squares in the top and bottom rows of a Karnaugh map are considered adjacent if they are in the same column (see Figure 3.16—squares 12 and 14).

3. Squares in the far left and far right of a Karnaugh map are considered adjacent if they are in the same row (see Figure 3.16—squares 2 and 10).

4. Don't care conditions for switching networks, which mean a specified input can't occur, are designated in the minterm and maxterm expansion by an X followed by the terms that can't occur in parentheses (see Figure 3.16(a)).

5. Don't care conditions are marked with an X in the specified square and may be grouped together with the 1s in a minterm (0s in a maxterm expansion) or ignored (see Figure 3.16(b)).

6. It is often useful to show the squares in which a variable will have a value of 1 (0 in the case of maxterms) with the use of brackets.

(a) Minterm Expansion

$f(A, B, C, D) = \Sigma m(0, 3, 7, 8, 10, 11, 12, 14, 15) + X(2, 5, 9)$

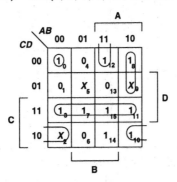

(b) Karnaugh Map

Figure 3.16 Karnaugh Map of Minterm Expansion

41

The reason we group squares together in Karnaugh maps for the purpose of circuit maximization, is shown in the following example.

EXAMPLE

Simplify F together with its don't care conditions in

(a) sum of products form

(b) product of sums form

$$F(A,B,C,D) = \sum m(0,1,2,8,9,12,13) + X(10,11,14,15)$$

F is simplified with a four variable K-map. Each don't care minterm can be treated as a 0 or a 1, whichever can help minimize F the most.

(a) The K-map is drawn with Xs representing don't care F minterms of 8, 9, 12, and 13 and don't cares treated as 1s at 10, 11, 14, and 15 combine to form A. F minterms at 0, 1, 8, and 9 combine to form $B'C'$. F minterms at 0, 2, and 8 and a don't care treated as a 1 at 10 combine to form $B'D'$. Thus, using sum of products,

$$F = A + B'C' + B'D'$$

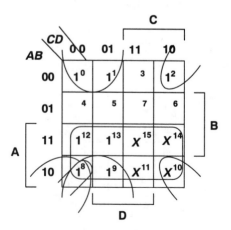

Figure 3.17

42

(b) Use the K-map of part a, but now minimize F' with the aid of the don't cares, and then use DeMorgan's Law to change F' to the product of sums form.

Thus,

$$F' = A'B + CD$$

Applying DeMorgan's Law gives the product of sums form

$$F = (A + B') \cdot (C' + D')$$

CHAPTER 4

Switching Circuits

The development of the transistor at Bell Laboratories in the late 1940s—which led to physicist William Shockley winning the Nobel Prize for his part in the development of the first silicon transistor—was a major breakthrough.

Today thousands and even millions of electronic components are integrated into a single chip using semiconductor technology. Engineers design computers by putting together chips containing many logic gates and other components. However, it is still important for the computer scientist to understand how these individual components interact with each other to form switching circuits, the subject of this chapter.

4.1 Semiconductor Theory

In order to analyze and design combinational circuits it is important to have an intuitive grasp of the circuit physics of semiconductors. If a designer has an intuitive feel for why logic gates behave the way they do, he will be more likely to spot potential trouble spots. These potential trouble spots can then be selected for more rigorous analysis (see first example in section 4.2 *Combination Circuits*).

Copper is an excellent conductor. The reason for this is that it has only one electron in its outer orbit. It has 29 electrons altogether with its first, second, and third orbits having their full complement of 2, 8, and 18, respectively.

44

The lone electrons in the outer orbits of copper atoms are loosely bound, so when an electric potential is applied these loosely bound electrons will form an electric current as they hop from atom to atom.

Insulators like plastic or ceramics will not conduct an electric current under normal conditions. The electrons in their outer orbits are tightly bound to the nucleus.

Semiconductors such as germanium or silicon are neither good conductors nor insulators. A silicon atom has 14 electrons, with its inner orbits having their full complement of 2 and 8 electrons, respectively. A silicon's outer orbit has 4 electrons which are neither tightly nor loosely bound to the nucleus.

The atoms of silicon are locked together in crystalline form (see Figure 4.1(a)) with each of the four electrons in its outer orbit shared with four adjacent atoms. When silicon is doped with a pentavalent (five electrons in its outer orbit) material such as arsenic, an N-type material results (see Figure 4.1(b)). The fifth electron in arsenic's outer shell does not interlock with the surrounding atoms and is thus loosely bound and will drift to surrounding atoms allowing an electric current to flow.

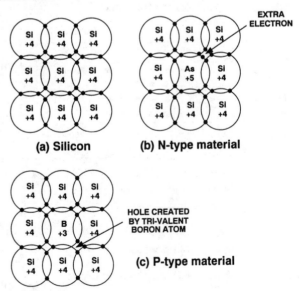

(a) Silicon   (b) N-type material

(c) P-type material

Figure 4.1 Atomic Structure of Semiconductor Material

When silicon is doped with a tri-valent material such as boron, a p-type material results (see Figure 4.1(c)), with the boron atom forming what is called a hole. The holes in a p-type material will also drift from atom to atom, thus allowing an electric current as the resulting freed-up electrons flow in the direction of a positive charge.

When tiny blocks of p-type material and n-type material are joined together we have a device with unique electrical characteristics. The pn-junction forms a depletion zone (see Figure 4.2(a)) when electrons from the n-type material flow over to fill holes in the p-type material. This depletion zone represents a barrier to electric currents that can be overcome with a small voltage—about .7V.

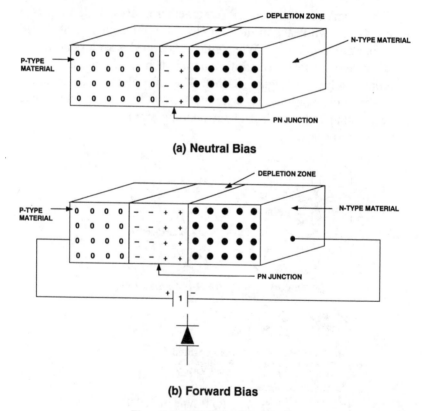

(a) Neutral Bias

(b) Forward Bias

Figure 4.2 The Junction Diode

However when a reverse bias voltage is applied to the pn-junction (see Figure 4.2(b)), the depletion zone only increases in size as more electrons from the n-side of the junction flow into the p-side to fill more holes. This barrier can only be overcome when high voltage creates what is called the avalanche effect. When a forward bias is applied, current will flow with a small voltage drop across the junction. This device, which only allows current in one direction, is called a diode.

Diodes can be used to form AND and OR gates as seen in the next two examples.

EXAMPLE

Using positive logic, determine the logic function represented by the diode circuit of Figure 4.3.

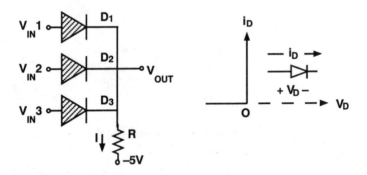

Figure 4.3   Figure 4.4

The ideal voltage-current characteristic of a diode is shown in Figure 4.4. The diode conducts when V_D is positive and acts as an insulator when V_D is negative. Hence, the diode is similar to a valve which lets current flow in only one direction.

As can be seen in Figure 4.3, when all inputs are high (greater than $-5V$) the diodes conduct, there is a large positive current in R, and the output voltage is greater than $-5V$.

When only one or two inputs are high, those diodes corresponding to the high inputs conduct and those diodes corresponding to the

47

low inputs (less than or equal to –5V) act as insulators. The conducting diode(s) pass current to the resistor R, forming a voltage drop. Hence, the output voltage is greater than –5V.

When all inputs are low (less than or equal to –5V), all the diodes acts as insulators and there is no current in resistor R; hence, the output voltage is –5V. From this information it is seen that the output is low only when all of the inputs are low. Tabulating this result, we get:

$V_{IN\,1}$	$V_{IN\,2}$	$V_{IN\,3}$	V_{OUT}
L	L	L	L
L	L	H	H
L	H	L	H
L	H	H	H
H	L	L	H
H	L	H	H
H	H	L	H
H	H	H	H

Table 4.1

It is evident that this table represents an OR gate.

EXAMPLE

Using positive logic, show that the diode circuit of Figure 4.5 represents a three-input AND gate.

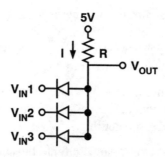

Figure 4.5

48

A diode is similar to a valve which lets current flow in only one direction. In Figure 4.5 it is seen that when all inputs are low (OV) all diodes conduct. This action brings V_{OUT} to the same voltage as $V_{IN\ N}$, hence, V_{OUT} is low.

When one or two inputs are high ($\geq$ 5V), any diodes corresponding to the low inputs conduct and any diodes corresponding to the high inputs act as insulators. Hence, the diodes that conduct bring V_{out} to the low voltage.

The diodes that are insulators have no effect on the output voltage. When all inputs are high, all of the diodes act as insulators and only then will the output voltage be high.

From this information, it is seen that the output is high only when all of the inputs are high. Using positive logic, this is seen to be an AND gate.

A bipolar npn junction transistor is shown in Figure 4.6. This type of transistor consists of a thin section of lightly doped p-type material between two blocks of heavily doped n-type material. When a positive voltage is applied to the base and collector, and a negative voltage is applied to the emitter, the forward bias across the pn junction causes a small current to flow from the emitter to the base. (Current flows in the opposite direction of a forward bias, from negative to positive.) This causes the np junction barrier to break down and a much larger current to flow from the emitter to the collector. Thus, a transmitter is much like a switch when voltage is applied to the base.

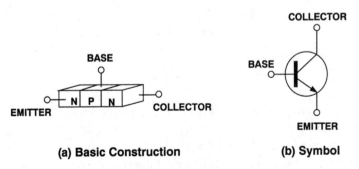

(a) Basic Construction   **(b) Symbol**

Figure 4.6 *DMPN* **Bipolar Transistor**

A bipolar pnp junction transistor works on a similar principle except the collector is connected to a negative voltage and the emitter to a positive.

The example below shows how diodes and transistors can be used to form a NAND gate.

EXAMPLE

Using positive logic, show that the diode-transistor circuit of Figure 4.7 represents a three-input NAND gate.

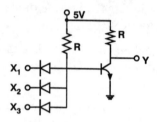

Figure 4.7

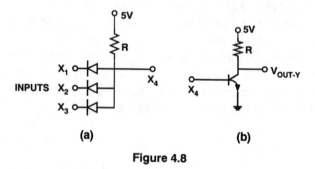

(a)   (b)

Figure 4.8

The circuit is broken down into two "sub-circuits": Figure 4.8(a) and (b).

In sub-circuit a, Figure 4.8(a), if any of the inputs are low, its corresponding diode will conduct, pulling the output X_4 low. If all the inputs are high ($\geq 5V$), none of the diodes will conduct, leaving the output X_4 high (5V). The truth table of Table 4.2 illustrates subcircuit a's action, that of an AND gate.

Inputs			Outputs
X_1	X_2	X_3	X_4
L	L	L	L
L	L	H	L
L	H	L	L
L	H	H	L
H	L	L	L
H	L	H	L
H	H	L	L
H	H	H	H

Table 4.2

In subcircuit b, Figure 4.8(b), the transistor acts as a switch, conducting when X_4 is high (> 7V), and open when X_4 is low (OV). When X_4 is high the transistor is conducting and the output Y is pulled low. When X_4 is low the transistor is open and Y floats to 5V (high). Thus, subcircuit b acts as an inverter and the whole circuit, whose truth table is shown in Table 4.3, acts as a NAND gate.

INPUTS			X_4	$Y_{(OUTPUT)}$
X_1	X_2	X_3		
L	L	L	L	H
L	L	H	L	H
L	H	L	L	H
L	H	H	L	H
H	L	L	L	H
H	L	H	L	H
H	H	L	L	H
H	H	H	H	L

Table 4.3

A complementary metal-oxide semiconductor (CMOS) combines both PMOS and NMOS transistors in a single gate as shown in Figure 4.12. Because CMOS circuits connect pairs of complementary transistors in series—one transistor is always off preventing current flow—these circuits draw virtually no drain current, and thus extremely low power is dissipated except when switching from state to state.

The previous three examples showed a type of gate that uses DTL or diode-transistor logic. TTL, or transistor-transistor logic, basically replaces the diode's inputs of DTL with a transistor. Figure 4.9 shows a TTL NAND gate.

If all three inputs (A, B, C) in the above figure are high, there is enough reverse leakage current from Q into the base of Q_2 to switch Q_2 on, because it only requires a small amount of base current to switch on a transistor. Because Q_2 is on, Q_4 will be off, and Q_3 will be on, resulting in a logic zero output. For all other input combinations the output will be logic 1.

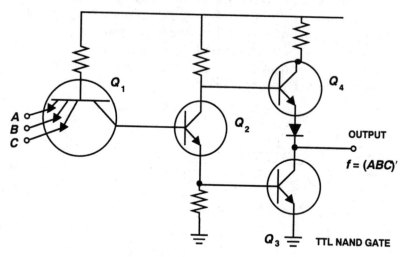

Figure 4.9

Field-effect transistors (FETs) are usually constructed using metal-oxide semiconductor (MOS) technology. A FET's source, drain, and gate is analogous to the emitter, collector, and base sections of a bipolar transistor.

52

The most important difference between the FET and the bipolar transmitter is that there is no flow through the gate of a FET while there is current flow through the base of a bipolar transistor. The NMOS FET shown in Figure 4.11(a) has a thin layer of silicon dioxide insulation between the gate and the underlying p-type material. When positive potential on the gate is increased past a certain threshold, enough electrons accumulate on the surface of the p-type material so in effect the p-type near the gate becomes n-type. This allows a current to flow from source to drain. The PMOS FET shown in Figure 4.11(b) works the same way except the gate is negatively charged.

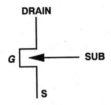

Figure 4.10 FET Schematic Symbol

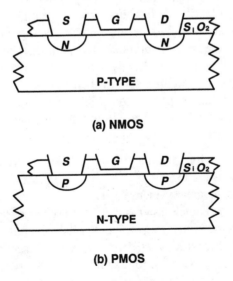

(a) NMOS

(b) PMOS

Figure 4.11 Field-Effect Transistor

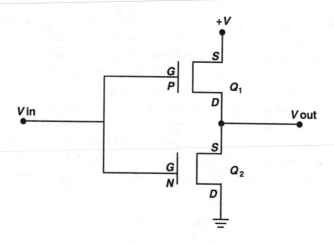

Figure 4.12 CMOS Inverter

Another important logic family is ECL or emitter-coupled logic. We won't study ECL in detail, except to point out that it is very fast and its power requirements are extremely high.

There are many logic families, but the three most important are TTL, CMOS, and ECL. Throughout most of the eighties, CMOS was used for personal computers because it had low power requirements and was less expensive to produce. Its main disadvantage was its slower switching speeds. TTL was used for mid-size computers because it had faster switching speeds than CMOS, higher power requirements, and higher production costs. ECL was used for mainframe and supercomputers because it was much faster, had extremely high power requirements, and was much more expensive to produce.

As semiconductor technology evolved, engineers and computer scientists found ways to pack more and more CMOS circuits onto a single chip and to greatly increase its switching speeds. Part of the reason CMOS is so much faster is that its dense packaging reduces the distance an electric signal must travel. CMOS technology has largely replaced TTL for most integrated circuits, and most mid-size computers use CMOS circuits. IBM, for example, is in the process of replacing its line of mainframe computers, which use ECL, with CMOS mainframes. Most supercomputers, however, still use ECL.

4.2 Combination Circuits

4.2.1 Combinational Circuit Analysis

As pointed out in the previous section, if the circuit designer has an intuitive feel for why a type of gate behaves the way it does, he will more likely be able to spot potential trouble spots. These potential trouble spots can then be selected for more rigorous analysis.

The example below shows how Boolean Algebra techniques can be used to analyze combinational circuits. The example after it will show the correct form of the circuits.

EXAMPLE

What is wrong with each of the following gate representations?

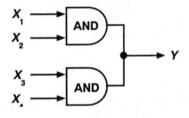

Figure 4.13

(a) This is an example of the incorrect assumption that a single variable may be controlled simultaneously from two or more elements whose outputs are inconsistent. Even though the definition of a gate structure is fulfilled—a set of elements with given behaviors and a set of couplings between elements—the contradictions inherent in the structure make its analysis meaningless. For example, if $X_1 = X_2 = 0$ and $X_3 = X_4 = 1$, then Y could be either 1 or 0.

(b) Although a circuit may contain dependency loops, this circuit contains a closed loop of inconsistent dependency in which a variable Y depends upon another variable X in such a way that two different values of Y are required simultaneously. This example fails for $Y = 0$ and $X = 1$ because Y must also be equal to 1 now.

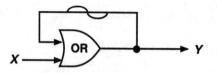

Figure 4.14

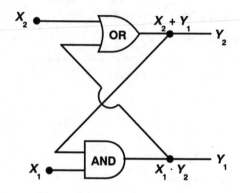

Figure 4.15

(c) Let us represent the output in terms of a pair of simultaneous Boolean equations:

$$Y_1 = X_1 \cdot Y_2$$
$$Y_2 = X_2 + Y_1$$

When solving these equations for Y_1 and Y_2 by substitution, we obtain either of two sets of equations:

$$Y_1 = Y_2 \cdot X_1$$
$$Y_2 = X_2 \qquad \text{(a)}$$

or

$$Y_1 = X_1$$
$$Y_2 = X_2 \cdot X_1 \qquad \text{(b)}$$

If we begin with $X_2 = 0$ and $X_1 = 1$, set (a) gives $Y_1 = Y_2 = 0$, but set (b) gives $Y_1 = Y_2 = 1$. With this state, the response of the circuit is ambiguous.

EXAMPLE

In the preceding problem, what would be correct forms for the circuits in parts (a) and (b)?

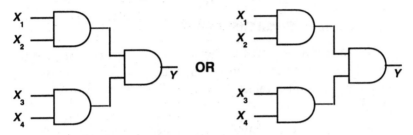

OR

Figure 4.16

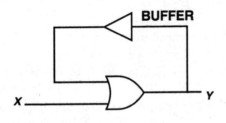

Figure 4.17

(a) For this circuit we would feed the outputs of the two AND gates into a second level AND or OR gate as shown in Figure 4.16.

(b) For this circuit the output Y of the OR gate can be fed back into one of its inputs by passing the output Y through a better amplifier. The advantages of using the buffer (with amplification >1 or <1) are listed below:

   (i)   It matches the output impedance of the OR gate to the input impedance of the OR gate.

   (ii) It balances any phase differences in the signals between the output side and the input side of the gate.

(iii) It also facilitates amplification or attenuation of the signal fed back from the output to the input so that the amount of signal fed back is the right amount. The possible circuit as shown in Figure 4.17.

4.2.2 Combinational Circuit Design

The switching networks in Chapter 3 had only one output. However, when a circuit is designed it may be necessary to have many outputs with possible values of 0 or 1. This is shown in the next example.

The circuit designer often also derives his specifications from a more general description, such as in the form of a word problem. This is also shown in the following example.

EXAMPLE

A combinational system is to receive a decimal value encoded according to code I. It also receives a control signal, J, that affects the output of the system. When J is TRUE, the input is converted to its equivalent in code II. When J is FALSE the output is chosen from code III. Design the combinational system for implementing this process. Consider both sum of products (SOP) and product of sums (POS) forms.

Minterm	Code I				Code II				Code III			
	A	B	C	D	W	X	Y	Z	W	X	Y	Z
1	0	0	0	1	0	0	0	0	0	0	1	1
2	0	0	1	0	0	0	0	1	0	1	0	0
4	0	1	0	0	0	0	1	0	0	1	0	1
8	1	0	0	0	0	0	1	1	0	1	1	0
9	1	0	0	1	0	1	0	0	0	1	1	1
10	1	0	1	0	0	1	0	1	1	0	0	0
12	1	1	0	0	0	1	1	0	1	0	0	1
13	1	1	0	1	0	1	1	1	1	0	1	0
14	1	1	1	0	1	0	0	0	1	0	1	1
15	1	1	1	1	1	0	0	1	1	1	0	0

Table 4.4

A five variable K-map is used to minimize each output. Notice that there are don't care minterms, namely, 0, 3, 5, 6, 7, and 11. Half of the K-map is used to $J = 1$ and the other half for $J = 0$. A K-map is drawn for each output W, X, Y, and Z.

It is seen from the W K-map that $W = \bar{J}AB + BC + \bar{J}AC$ and in the POS form

$$W = (A)(\bar{J} + \bar{A} + C)(\bar{A} + B + C)(\bar{J} + D + B).$$

Similarly:

$$X = \bar{J}\,\bar{A}\,\bar{D} + A\bar{B}\,D + \bar{J}\,CD + JA\bar{B}\,\bar{C} + JA\bar{B}\,C\bar{D} + JAB\bar{C}$$

$$X = (\bar{J} + A)(A + \bar{D})(J + \bar{A} + \bar{B} + C)(J + \bar{A} + \bar{C} + D)$$

$$\quad (\bar{J} + B + C + D)(\bar{J} + \bar{A} + \bar{B} + \bar{C})$$

$$Y = \bar{J}\,\bar{C}\,D + JB\bar{C} + A\bar{B}\,\bar{C}\,\bar{D} + \bar{J}\,BC\bar{D}$$

$$Y = (\bar{J} + \bar{C})(\bar{C} + \bar{D})(B + \bar{C})(\bar{J} + B + C + \bar{D})(J + \bar{B} + C + D)$$

$$Z = JBD + JA\bar{B}\,\bar{D} + J\bar{B}\,C\bar{D} + \bar{J}\,\bar{B}\,D + \bar{J}\,B\bar{D}$$

$$Z = (J + \bar{B} + \bar{D})(J + \bar{A} + D + B)(J + B + \bar{C} + D)(\bar{J} + B + \bar{D})(\bar{J} + \bar{B} + D)$$

To decide which method would be cheapest to implement, SOP or POS, we will look at the number of gates required for implementation. The table of Figure 4.18 shows the number of gates needed to implement the SOP and the POS form of each variable.

It is seen from Figure 4.18 that W and Y are best expressed in the SOP form because the SOP form takes the least amount of gates. X and Z can be expressed in either SOP or POS form as both require the same number of gates. We will express X in POS form and Z in SOP form.

Figure 4.19 shows the circuit implementation with W, Y, and Z expressed in the SOP form and X in the POS form.

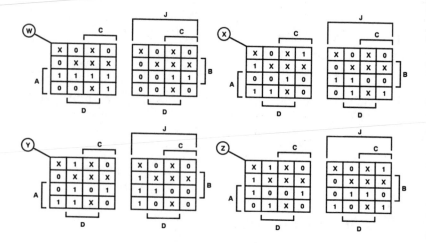

Variable	Gates	
	SOP	POS
W	4	5
X	7	7
Y	5	6
Z	6	6

Figure 4.18

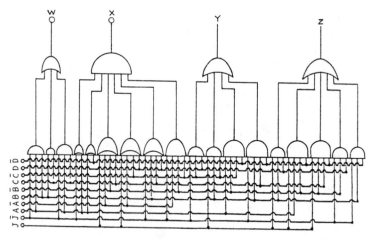

Figure 4.19

Encoders

An encoder is a device which converts raw binary inputs, usually from a peripheral device, into a binary number that is more easily handled by a computer. For example, if a computer key pad had 110 keys and if when each of them was pressed down a separate line showed a binary value of 1, it would be useful to encode these 110 different binary values into a 7-bit binary number before the computer received it.

The example below shows how to design a simple encoder with 8 input lines and a binary output of 3 bits.

EXAMPLE

Design an 8 × 3 encoder.

An encoder is a device with 2^n input lines (in this case 8) and n output lines (in this case 3). Only one of the input lines can be excited at any one time. The encoder generates on its output lines a code corresponding to the input line that was excited. The truth table for the 8 × 3 encoder is shown in Table 4.5. Bits I_0 through I_7 are the input lines and bits A_0 through A_2 are the output lines. A_0 is the most significant output bit; A_2 is the least significant output bit. From the truth table it is seen that

$$A_0 = I_4 + I_5 + I_6 + I_7$$
$$A_1 = I_2 + I_3 + I_6 + I_7$$
$$A_2 = I_1 + I_3 + I_5 + I_7$$

Inputs								Outputs		
I_0	I_1	I_2	I_3	I_4	I_5	I_6	I_7	A_0	A_1	A_2
1	0	0	0	0	0	0	0	0	0	0
0	1	0	0	0	0	0	0	0	0	1
0	0	1	0	0	0	0	0	0	1	0
0	0	0	1	0	0	0	0	0	1	1
0	0	0	0	1	0	0	0	1	0	0
0	0	0	0	0	1	0	0	1	0	1
0	0	0	0	0	0	1	0	1	1	0
0	0	0	0	0	0	0	1	1	1	1

Table 4.5

61

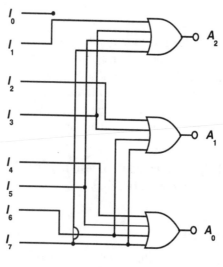

Figure 4.20

The logic diagram of the encoder is obtained from these equations. Figure 4.20 shows the encoder.

Decoders

A decoder is a digital function that converts binary information from one coded form to another. For example, a BCD-to-seven-segment decoder connects a decimal digit in BCD (binary-coded decimal) into seven outputs for the selection of seven segments to display a decimal digit. Digital clocks with seven-segment displays employ these kind of decoders.

More general purpose decoders are called n-to-2^n line decoders. Their purpose is to generate the 2^n minterms of n input variables. These decoders form the combinational logic with n input variables and 2^n output variables. For each binary input combination of 1s and 0s there is one, and only one, output line that assumes the value of 1. The example below shows how to design a 5-to-2^5 or 5 × 32 decoder.

EXAMPLE

Design a 5 × 32 decoder using four 3 × 8 decoders (with enable inputs) and one 2 × 4 decoder.

A decoder is a digital device with n input lines and 2^n output lines. The truth table and logic diagram for a 2×4 decoder is shown in Figure 4.21 below.

X	Y	Z_0	Z_1	Z_2	Z_3
0	0	1	0	0	0
0	1	0	1	0	0
1	0	0	0	1	0
1	1	0	0	0	1

(a) Truth Table

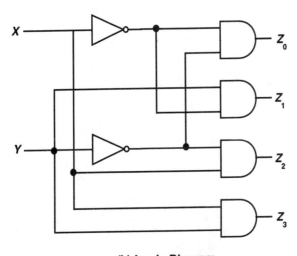

(b) Logic Diagram

Figure 4.21   2 × 4 Decoder

Sometimes we want a decoder's outputs to be all logic 0. To do this we design a decoder with an enable input. The logic diagram for a 3×8 decoder is shown in Figure 4.22 (a) and the block diagram in Figure 4.22 (b).

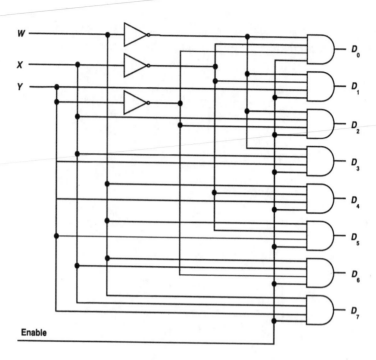

(a) Logic Diagram

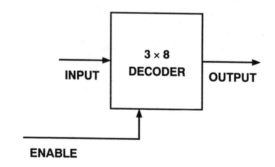

(b) Block Diagram

Figure 4.22   3 × 8 Decoder with Enable

Smaller decoders can be used as building blocks to construct much larger decoders. The block diagram for a 5×2^5 or 5×32

decoder is shown in Figure 4.23 with each of the four outputs of a 2 × 4 decoder connected to the enable inputs of four 3 × 8 decoders.

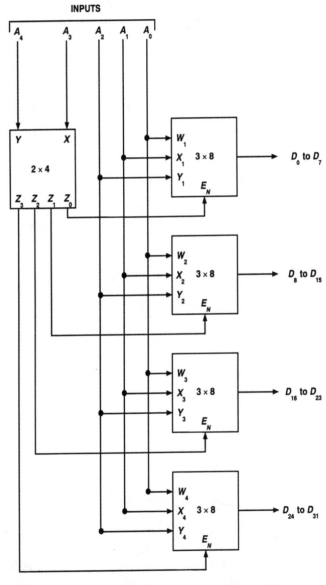

Figure 4.23   5 × 32 Decoder

Multiplexers

A digital multiplexer can be thought of as performing the inverse operation of a decoder. A multiplexer is a digital function that receives binary information from 2^n lines and transmits information on a single output line. A typical application would be to receive digitized voice data from several telephone lines and select one for transmission over a high-speed cable. Figure 4.24 shows a 4 × 1 multiplexer. Note that there are also two select lines; a 2^n × 1 multiplexer requires n select lines. Since this is a 4 · 1 or 2^2 × 1 multiplexer there are two select lines.

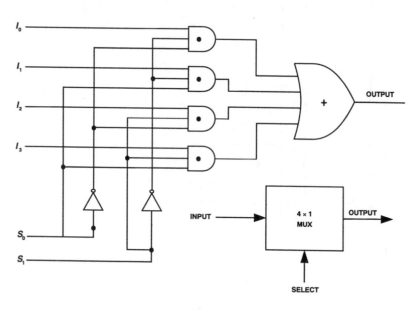

Figure 4.24 4 × 1 Multiplexer

4.3   Sequential Circuit Analysis

Sequential circuits have the property that the output depends not only on the present input but on the past sequence of inputs as well. This property requires some kind of "memory" capability. Flip-flops are the devices which provide "memory" for sequential circuits.

4.3.1 Flip-flops

Flip-flops have the ability to store a 0 or a 1. Figure 4.25 shows a basic flip-flop or latch. A latch is a basic circuit upon which other more complicated flip-flops can be constructed.

The crosscoupled connections in Figure 4.25 from Q and Q' back to the inputs of the NAND gates are called feedback paths. A NAND latch operates with both inputs high. When R is momentarily lowered to Q' and S remains a 1, Q is forced high and its feedback path causes Q' to become a 0. When both inputs go back to 1, Q and Q' retain their values, thus an R-S batch "holds" or latches on to 1 bit of memory. When S is momentarily lowered to 0, while R remains a 1, the same thing happens in reverse.

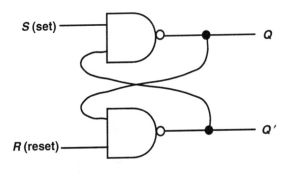

Figure 4.25 R-S latch

The state of a flip-flop is defined by its Q output, because the Q' output is always the complement of Q. When Q is 1 we say the flip-flop is in its set state, and when Q is 0 we say it is in its clear state.

Asynchronous sequential circuits are basically combinational circuits with feedback paths. Because feedback paths may at times become unstable, asynchronous systems are seldom used in computers. Synchronization of circuits which employ logic gates and flip-flops is achieved by a timing device called a clock-pulse generator. The output of a clock-pulse generator is shown in Figure 4.26. A typical pulse width could be about 100 nanoseconds or 100 billionths of a second.

Figure 4.26 Clock-Pulse

The clocked R-S flip-flop shown in Figure 4.27 will only respond to its R and S inputs when the clock-pulse is high. The graphic symbol for the R-S flip-flop is shown in Figure 4.28(b) and its state table is shown in Figure 4.28(a). We refer to $Q(t)$ as its present state and $Q(t + 1)$ as the next state. The last entry in the state table shows the main disadvantage of the R-S flip-flop; when $R = S = 1$ the state is ambiguous.

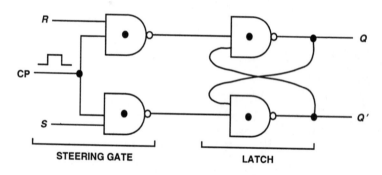

Figure 4.27 Logic Diagram of a Clocked R-S Flip-Flop

S	R	$Q(t + 1)$	Comments
0	0	$Q(t)$	No change
0	1	0	Clear
1	0	1	Set
1	1	?	Not allowed

(a) State Table

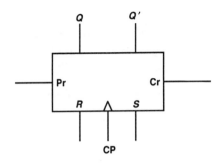

(b) Graphic Symbol

Figure 4.28 *R-S* **Flip-Flop**

There are two types of flip-flops in use today: edge triggered and pulse triggered. These can be further subdivided into positive-edge triggered and negative-edge triggered. The *R-S* flip-flop shown in Figure 4.27 changes state on the rising or positive edge of the clock-pulse, although this has nothing to do with why we define it as an *R-S* type of flip-flop. The type of flip-flop is defined by its state table. We say that the flip-flop shown in Figure 4.27 is a positive-edge triggered *R-S* flip-flop.

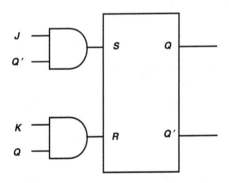

Figure 4.29 Diagram of *J-K* **Flip-Flop**

The *J-K* flip-flop is an attempt to remove the ambiguity from the *R-S* flip-flop. The easiest way to think of a *J-K* flip-flop is as an *R-S* flip-flop with the *Q* and *Q'* outputs looped back and ANDed with the inputs as shown in Figure 4.29. Though the actual internal design may vary, what makes it a *J-K* flip-flop is that the $J = 1$, $K = 1$ condition is determinate (see Figure 4.30(a)). However, very fast circuits may oscillate and ambiguity can still occur.

J	K	$Q(t+1)$	Comments
0	0	$Q(t)$	No change
0	1	0	Clear
1	0	1	Set
1	1	$Q'(t)$	Toggle

(a) State Table

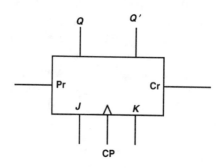

(b) Graphic Symbol

Figure 4.30 J-K Flip-Flop

The Pr and Cr inputs in Figure 4.32(b), which shows the graphic symbol of a *J-K*, will preset (set to 1) or clear to 0, overriding the clock-pulse.

The *J-K* master-slave flip-flop can be thought of as two *J-K* flip-flops in cascade, with the inputs of the slave being the outputs of the master ANDed with the inverted clock-pulse in Figure 4.31, although, again, the actual internal design may vary. The master is triggered by a positive edge and the slave by a negative edge. This inhibits any possibility of output oscillation. Because it takes a full clock-pulse to change state, we call this a pulse-triggered flip-flop.

70

Since the state table is (see Figure 4.32(a)) the same as a *J-K* flip-flop, the *J-K* master-slave flip-flop is still a *J-K* flip-flop, only pulse-triggered!

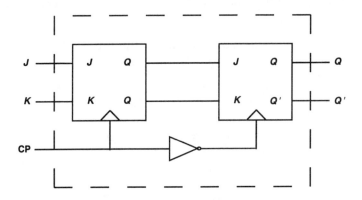

Figure 4.31 *J-K* Master-Slave Flip-Flop

J	K	$Q(t+1)$	Comments
0	0	$Q(t)$	No change
0	1	0	Clear
1	0	1	Set
1	1	$Q'(t)$	Toggle

(a) State Table

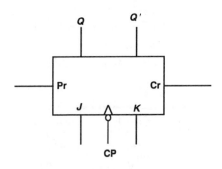

(b) Graphic Symbol

Figure 4.32 *J-K* Master-Slave Flip-Flop

71

The *D* (delay) flip-flop is a simple flip-flop; when triggered by a clock input, *Q* is the same as the *D* input. Note the inversion symbol on its graphic symbol in Figure 4.33(b), which indicates a negative-edge triggered *D* flip-flop. The *D* flip-flop is used to delay a signal for timing purposes.

D	Q(t + 1)	Comments
0	Q(t)	Set
0	0	Clear

(a) State Table

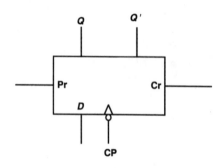

(b) Graphic Symbol

Figure 4.33 *D* Flip-Flop

The *T* flip-flop is another simple flip-flop which simply toggles on each clock-pulse, as long as the *T* input is high. A *J-K* flip-flop can be made into a *T* flip-flop simply by connecting the *J* and *K* lines. The *J-K* flip-flop is the most versatile and the most used in sequential circuits.

T	Q(t + 1)	Comments
1	Q(t)	Toggle
0	0(t)	No change

(a) State Table

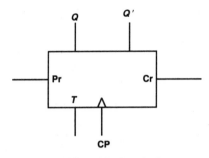

(b) Graphic Symbol

Figure 4.34 *T* Flip-Flop

4.3.2 Excitation Equations

The excitation equation of a flip-flop is a Boolean function which represents the conditions which cause the next state of the flip-flop to be set. For example, if the *D* input of a *D* flip-flop is *a*1, on the next state transition, the *D* flip-flop will be set, irregardless of its present state. The excitation equation for a *D* flip-flop is:

$$\overrightarrow{Q} = D,$$

with the arrow above the *Q* representing "next transition of *Q*."

The example below shows how to derive excitation equations using Karnaugh maps.

EXAMPLE

Derive the excitation equation of a *J-K* flip-flop.

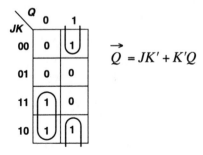

$$\overrightarrow{Q} = JK' + K'Q$$

Figure 4.35

73

The excitation equations for the T and R-S flip-flops are shown below:

$$\overrightarrow{Q} = TQ' + T'Q$$
$$\overrightarrow{Q} = R + S'Q$$

4.4 Sequential Circuit Design

The design of sequential circuits can be a very complicated task. However, if the design procedure follows the outline we will describe in the next three sections, it can be done methodically and systematically.

4.4.1 State Diagrams

The usual procedure for designing a sequential circuit is to first formulate the behavior of the circuit in the form of a state diagram,

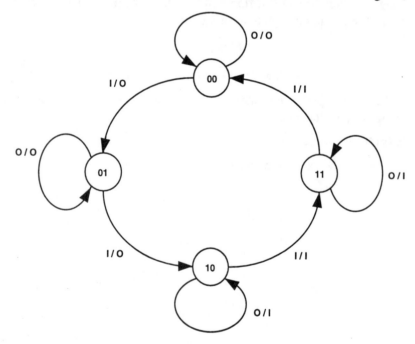

Figure 4.36 State Diagram

as shown in Figure 4.36. The binary number inside the circles indicates the present state of the circuit flip-flops. The directed lines are labeled with two binary numbers separated by slashes. The input number that caused the slash is labeled first and the number after the slash is the output.

If the specifications for a sequential circuit call for a 2-bit binary counter which output the most significant bit of the present state of the counter and increment when the input is 1, it would be represented by the state diagram shown in Figure 4.36.

4.4.2 State Tables

When designing a sequential circuit, once a state diagram has been created, the next step is to transfer the information into a state table. State tables of sequential circuits are conceptually very similar to the state tables of flip-flops we studied earlier.

A sequential circuit can be divided into two parts. The first part constitutes a combinational circuit made up of logic gates. The second part consists of flip-flops in which the present state of the circuit is stored.

A state table for a sequential circuit is divided into three sections. The first section shows the inputs. Since the present state of the flip-flops are also inputs of the combinational part of the circuit, they also go in the first section. The second section shows the next state of the sequential circuit (the state of the flip-flops after the next clock-pulse). The third section shows the outputs of the circuit for the present state.

Table 4.6 shows a state table that was created by transferring the information from the state diagram of the binary counter in the previous section.

Present State Input			Next State		Output
A	B	Y	A	B	Z
0	0	0	0	0	0
0	0	1	0	1	0
0	1	0	0	1	0
0	1	1	1	0	0
1	0	0	1	0	1
1	0	1	1	1	1
1	1	0	1	1	1
1	1	1	0	0	1

Table 4.6 State Table

4.4.3 Synchronous Sequential Circuit

This section will show how to complete the design of a synchronous sequential circuit after a state diagram and state table have been created from the specifications of the circuit behavior.

The next step, following our example from the previous two sections of a binary counter, is to create an excitation table for the circuit's flip-flops. A binary counter requires two flip-flops, and we have already labeled them flip-flop A and flip-flop B in the previous section. If we employ J-K flip-flops, we can label the inputs of the flip-flops JA, KA, JB, and KB.

If we look at the fourth row of Table 4.6, we can see that there is a transition from 0 to 1 for flip-flop A, thus the input for flip-flop A in the fourth row of our excitation table (see Table 4.7) must show a 1 for JA. However, it doesn't matter what input KA is in the fourth row, so we label it X for don't care. The other entries for Table 4.6 are made in a similar manner.

Flip-Flop		Inputs	
JA	KA	JB	KB
0	X	0	X
0	X	1	X
0	X	X	0
1	X	X	1
X	0	0	X
X	0	1	X
X	0	X	0
X	1	X	1

Table 4.7 Excitation Table

Once we have entered all of our flip-flop input conditions into an excitation table, we can derive a Boolean function for each flip-flop input by using Karnaugh maps.

The logic flow of a sequential circuit is: the outputs of the flip-flops are looped around and become inputs back into the circuit, along with the external inputs. These inputs go into the combinational part of the circuit, which is designed by Karnaugh maps as shown in Figure 4.37. The outputs of the combinational part become inputs back into the flip-flops or memory part.

The circuit flip-flops change state, depending on their current inputs, when there is a clock-pulse. The loop-backs into the same state, in Figure 4.36, represent a clock-pulse with no flip-flop changing state. The transition from one state to another in Figure 4.36 represent a clock-pulse with one or more flip-flops changing state.

In Figure 4.37 the inputs are taken from the state table (Table 4.6) and are represented at the upper left-hand corner of each Karnaugh map and the upper right-hand side of each Boolean equation. The flip-flop input conditions (which are outputs of the combinational part) are taken from the excitation table (Table 4.7) and are represented by an entry of 0, 1, or X in each square of the Karnaugh maps and the left-hand side of each Boolean equation in Figure 4.37.

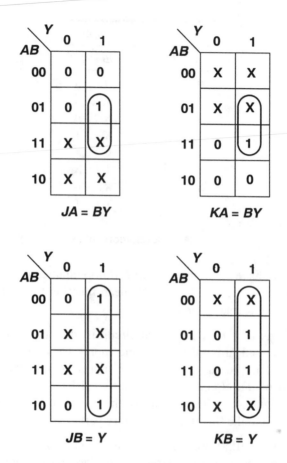

Figure 4.37 Maps for Combinational Circuit of Counter

It is important to understand that since the outputs of the flip-flops are inputs back into the sequential circuit, a master-slave J-K type of flip-flop should be used so the slave can hold the output while the master is receiving the next input.

Getting back to the design of our binary counter, once the Boolean function for the inputs of each flip-flop has been derived, it is easy to complete our design. Note that the input y, which is the most significant digit of the binary counter, does not require any combinational logic in this example. Normally outputs of sequential circuits are part of the combinational part of the circuit and there is a Boolean expression derived for each output. Figure 4.38 shows the completed design of the binary counter.

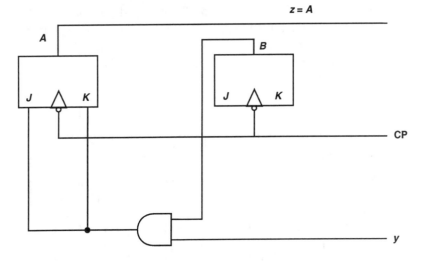

Figure 4.38 Binary Counter

Synchronous sequential circuits usually perform some kind of control function for a computer, and they can be very complex. The trick is to break them down into subcircuits which can be designed systematically. The designer of the circuit we have just completed would not have to worry about what functions input y and output z provided for a much larger sequential circuit, thus making his task much easier.

4.4.4 Register

A register is a group of flip-flops together with gates that affect the flip-flops' transition. A register may be used to store a binary number that will later have a binary arithmetic operation performed on it, it may contain a memory address, or it may be used for some other purpose such as a logical operation.

A 4-bit register that uses R-S flip-flops is shown in Figure 4.39. The data inputs are I_1, I_2, I_3, and I_4. The control inputs are CP (clock-pulse), load, and clear. The data outputs are A_1, A_2, A_3, and A_4.

The clock-pulse is common to all four flip-flops and consists of continuous pulses. The circle under the triangle of each flip-flop indicates that these are negative-edge triggered flip-flops.

The load input is connected to all four flip-flops via the AND gates. When Load is 0 the inputs to each R and S is 0, and Q remains in the previous state. When Load is 1 the inputs to each R and S are I_N and I_n', thus each output A_n will show the value of I_n'.

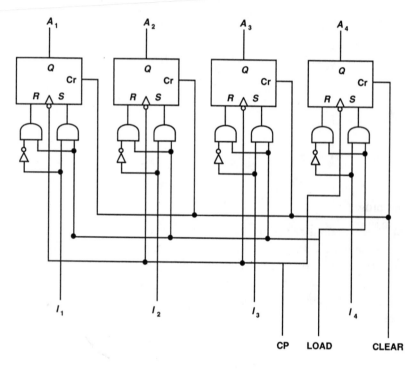

Figure 4.39 4-Bit Register

The design of a register is usually straightforward enough that it doesn't require the techniques of using a state diagram, state table, and excitation table. However, it is usually part of a larger sequential circuit that does require those techniques.

CHAPTER 5

Computer Architecture

Computer architecture is the structural organization of the computer. It is made up of the basic building blocks from which computers are structured such as registers, multiplexers, decoders, arithmetic units, memory cells, and the like.

Computer architecture is often defined as that part of the hardware the programmer is interested in. This is a good definition, although a computer architect is an engineer concerned with hardware design.

Computer scientists who are involved in the design of system dependent software, such as operating systems and compilers, are more likely to be interested in computer architecture than application programmers. Application programmers, however, often study the architecture of a computer to improve the efficiency of their design.

5.1 Basic Terms

Memory Unit—The memory unit of a computer is made up of random access memory (RAM) which is discussed in the next section. The memory is connected to the central processing unit (CPU) by address lines and data lines. The memory unit is organized into words, which are multiples of 1, 2, 4, or 8 bytes.

Registers—The chief differences between registers and words in memory are: registers are much fewer in number, registers are "on-board" or part of the CPU, and registers are much faster to access.

Central Processing Unit—The CPU is responsible for the timing and control of the computer, and for the execution of the machine language instructions which are stored in memory. The CPU is made up of registers, the control unit, and the arithmetic logic unit (ALU).

Arithmetic Logic Unit—The ALU is made up of the arithmetic unit and the logic unit. The arithmetic unit is constructed from parallel adders, sometimes parallel subtractors, and one or more shift registers to facilitate multiplication and division. The logic unit performs logic operations such as AND, OR, or complement (inverse). The difference between these operations and the ones we have studied is that the logic operation is performed on each bit of a register. For example, the AND operation ANDs each of the corresponding bits of two different registers.

Input/Output (I/O)—There must be a way for the computer to communicate with the external world. It does this by performing input/output operations with peripheral devices such as printers, disk drives, monitors, etc.

5.2 Random Access Memory (RAM)

A tape drive is a serial access memory device. If a tape drive is accessing data at the beginning of a reel and then needs to access data near the end of the reel, it must unwind almost the entire reel, checking as it goes, to access the data.

A disk drive is a semi-random access memory device. The movable head goes directly to the track to be read or written to, but then waits while the disk spins to the sector containing the data to be accessed.

Random access memory (RAM) allows data to be accessed directly, regardless of its location. Data is stored in RAM in groups of bits called words. Each bit is stored in a memory cell which is the basic building block of a computer.

A logic diagram of a memory cell using R-S flip-flops is shown in Figure 5.1(a). When the Select line is high and the Read/Write line is low, a 1 or 0 at the Data-in input will be stored in the memory cell.

When both the Select line and the Read/Write lines are high, the Data-out line is enabled, allowing the memory cell to be read.

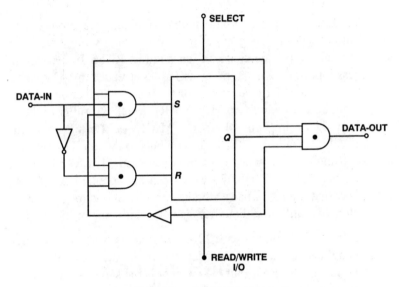

(a) Logic Diagram of Memory Cell

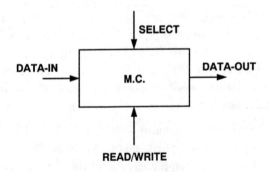

(b) Block Diagram

Figure 5.1 Memory Cell

Figure 5.1(b) shows the block diagram of a memory cell. Figure 5.2 shows how memory cells can be used as building blocks to design a 4 × 3 (4 bits per word, by 3 words) RAM using OR gates and a decoder. The logic diagram of the decoder is that of a 2×4 decoder which is shown in the example under *Decoders* in Chapter Four.

The address selection inputs shown in Figure 5.2 represent an important concept. The address of a word is a binary number which is used to refer to the location of a word in that RAM. If a RAM has 20 address inputs, then a computer will access (read from or write to) a word in that RAM by storing a 20 bit binary number in what is called the memory address register (MAR), which is similar to the 4-bit register shown in Figure 4.40. The MAR would in turn hold the 20 address lines leading to the address inputs to the appropriate high or low setting while a word of data is accessed. If a RAM has 20 address inputs, 2^{20} or 1,048,576 words can be stored in that RAM, and we say that the RAM has a storage capacity of one mega-word—mega refers to a million although 2^{20} is not exactly one million.

The decoder of a RAM with 20 address inputs is obviously much more complicated than the decoder shown in the example under *Decoders* in Chapter Four, but the concept is the same. Also, a MAR 20 bits wide would be more complicated than the 4-bit register shown in Figure 4.40, but the concept is very similar.

The RAM in Figure 5.2 has 3-bit words, if it had 4-bit words it would be a nibble. Two nibbles, or 8 bits, is a byte. Words in RAMs of actual computers are usually multiples of bytes, from 2 bytes (16 bits) up to 8 bytes (64 bits). If a RAM has a storage capacity of 1 mega-word and each word is 2 bytes long, then the RAM has a capacity of 2 mega-bytes.

The diagrams of the memory cell and RAM in Figures 5.1 and 5.2 do not show a clock-pulse input; however, the clock-pulse is assumed for the sake of simplicity. All of the building blocks which make up the architecture of a digital computer are synchronized by a clock, and the computer scientist should assume there is always a clock input.

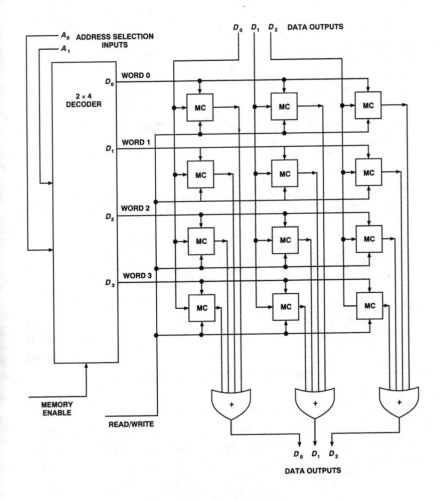

Figure 5.2 4 × 3 RAM

5.3 Full-Adder

The half-adder is a combinational circuit which performs the arithmetic addition of 2 bits. The sum output of the half-adder, whose sum is 1 if and only if one of the inputs is 1 and the other is 0, could be given by the Boolean expression:

$$(X \cdot Y') + (X' \cdot Y)$$

The carry output of a half-adder, which is 1 if and only if both inputs are 1, could be given by:

$$(X \cdot Y)$$

With these two Boolean expressions in mind, it is easy to design a half-adder as shown in Figure 5.3.

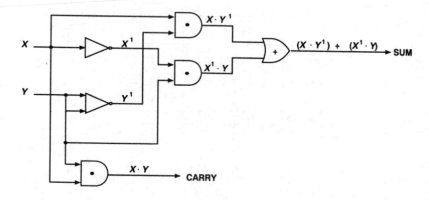

Figure 5.3 Diagram of Half-Adder

However, it takes two half-adders to perform binary addition, with the sum of the first half-adder and the carry from the previous bit becoming the inputs of the second half-adder and the carry outputs being ORed together.

It is easier to design a full-adder using EXCLUSIVE-OR gates to do the job. Figure 5.4(a) shows a full-adder which accepts the carry bit of a previous addition of two less significant bits and provides the carry for the next addition of two more significant bits.

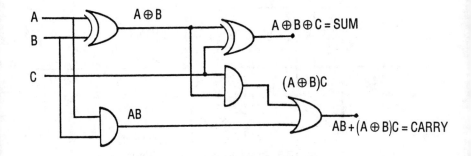

(a) Logic Diagram of Full-Adder

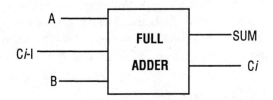

(b) Block Diagram

Figure 5.4 Full-Adder

To add two binary numbers of more than one digit we use a parallel adder. Figure 5.5 shows the block diagram of a parallel-adder capable of adding two 4-bit numbers. The parallel-adder in Figure 5.5 is simply a chain of four full-adders with carries connected.

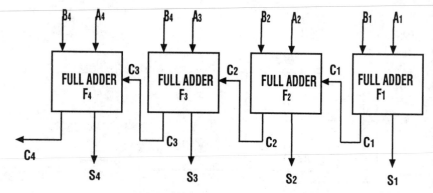

Figure 5.5 Parallel-Adder Block Diagram

The above parallel-adder uses what is called a cascade design, with the inputs allowed to propagate through the circuit until the addition is completed. Computers will often use adders with look-ahead carry generators so that true parallel addition can occur. Look-ahead carry generators allow addition of each bit simultaneously, in one clock cycle, without having to wait until the carry propagates through the chain of full-adders. Although we won't show one here for the sake of brevity, look-ahead carry generators are combinational circuits designed with the same techniques, such as Boolean Algebra, and are not especially sophisticated.

5.4   Full-Subtractor

A full-subtractor is a combinational circuit that performs a subtraction between two bits while taking into account the fact that a 1 may have been borrowed from by a lower significant position.

The logic diagram of a full-subtractor is surprisingly similar to the full-adder shown in Figure 5.5. Although we didn't show the design process of a full-adder, we will for a full-subtractor in the example below.

EXAMPLE

Design a full-subtractor by first obtaining Boolean functions for its difference and borrow outputs.

The three inputs represent the minuend, subtrahend, and previous

88

borrow, respectively. The two outputs represent the difference and next borrow.

A	B	C	Diff	Borrow
0	0	0	0	0
0	0	1	1	1
0	1	0	1	1
0	1	1	0	1
1	0	0	1	0
1	0	1	0	0
1	1	0	0	0
1	1	1	1	1

Table 5.1

Now use the Karnaugh maps of Figure 5.6 to find the logic equations.

$$\text{Difference} = AB'C' + A'BC$$
$$+ ABC + A'B'C$$
$$= A + B + C$$
(same as full-adder)

$$\text{Borrow} = A'B'C + A'BC'$$
$$+ BC$$
$$= A'[B'C + BC']$$
$$+ BC$$
$$= A'(B + C) + BC$$

DIFFERENCE

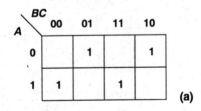

(a)

BORROW

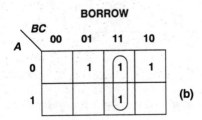

(b)

Figure 5.6

89

The Circuit Implementation of a full-subtractor is shown in Figure 5.7.

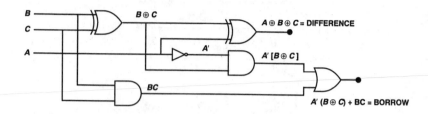

Figure 5.7

Because of the similarity of the full-subtractor and the full-adder, some use a single unit to perform both addition and subtraction. Figure 5.8 shows how a unit that performs both functions might be designed.

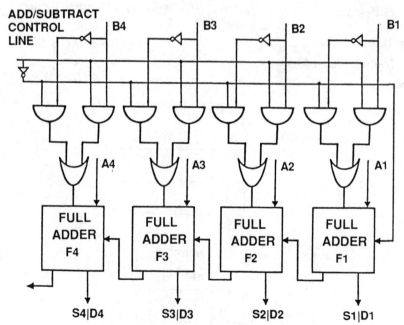

Figure 5.8 Parallel 4-Bit Adder-Subtractor

Computers will also perform subtraction by adding complements of binary numbers as was shown in Section 2.5.2, *Subtraction Using Binary Numbers.*

Again, although the clock-pulse is assumed and not shown in this section, all digital computers use clock-pulse to synchronize arithmetic operations. It would be a useful exercise for the reader to study the diagrams in this and the previous section and try to figure out where a clock input could be added.

5.5   Data Transfer

In a computer system it is desirable to be able to transfer data between any two registers. This means there must be a data path between each flip-flop in one register and the corresponding flip-flop in every other register. Consider, for example, a system with three registers as shown in Figure 5.9. If data can be transferred between any two of these registers, there are six data paths between registers. If each register consists of n flip-flops, there are $6n$ data paths.

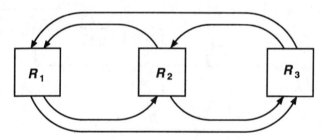

Figure 5.9 Transfer Between Three Registers

If the number of registers is equal to r then $(2^r - 1)n$ data paths, or lines, is required. These would lead to a horrendous increase in the complexity and the cost of the system. However, a data transfer system called a "bus system" can greatly simplify transmission between registers.

A group of wires that transmits binary information between registers is called a bus. This concept is analogous to commuter transportation that relies on buses rather than private cars.

A bus system is formed with a bus line (a group of wires), multiplexers, and decoders. Figure 5.10 shows how a group of 4 × 1 multiplexers selects the outputs of one of the registers for transmission onto the bus line. Figure 5.11 shows how decoders are used to select the register that receives the contents of the register selected by the multiplexers.

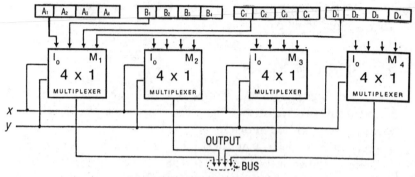

(a) Detailed Block Diagram

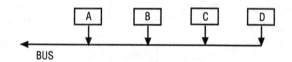

(b) Simplified Block Diagram

Figure 5.10 Bus System for Four Registers

If the data outputs of Register B were selected and Register RO was selected to receive the contents of Register B, the select lines to the multiplexers would be XY' and the select lines to the decoders would by $Z'W'$. The transfer of data could be symbolically represented by

$$XY' : \text{BUS} \leftarrow A, \; Z'W' : \text{RO} \leftarrow \text{BUS}$$

The fact that both transfers are done simultaneously, on the same clock cycle, is indicated by listing them on the same line. The above operation is what is called a micro-operation, which we will say more about in the next section.

When data is transferred from RAM to a register or from a register to RAM, the most straightforward way to address the memory location in RAM is with a memory address register (MAR) as described in Section 5.2 *Random Access Memory*. The use of a MAR is shown in Figure 5.11(a) with the contents of the word being transferred to or from the memory buffer register depending on whether a read or write has been enabled. If the operation was a read, then the word of data can be transferred to another register when the next micro-operative is performed.

A computer that allows any register to be used as an address register requires a more complicated design. A bus system that uses multiplexers, as shown in Figure 5.11(b), can be constructed, allowing any register to address RAM. Thus, one micro-operation and one clock cycle is saved on a read or write to RAM, because the address does not first have to be transferred to an MAR.

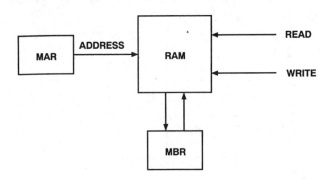

(a) Accessing RAM with a MAR

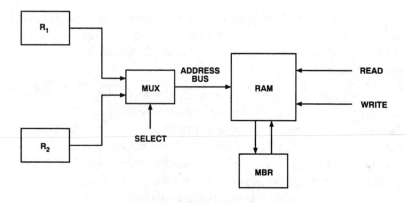

(b) Using an Address Bus

Figure 5.11 Methods of Addressing RAM

5.6 Summary of Computer Architecture

A computer's architecture is made up of the basic building blocks of a computer. There are three main subdivisions: the central processing unit (CPU), the memory unit, and the Input/Output (I/O) interface as shown in Figure 5.12.

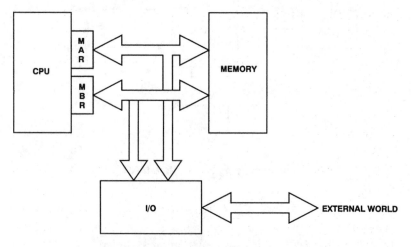

Figure 5.12 Organization of a Computer

The central processing unit consists of registers, the arithmetic logic unit, and the control unit. The contents of registers may include data that is being worked on by its current instruction, and the addresses in memory of instructions or data. The ALU is made up of full-adders, perhaps full-subtractors, and logic gates that allow Boolean operators to be performed on whole registers rather than a single bit.

The control unit transmits a clock-pulse which synchronizes the entire computer and also sends control signals to the ALU and the multiplexers and decoders of the bus system which transfers data between registers.

The memory unit is made up of random access memory and is connected to the memory address register (MAR) and the memory buffer register (MBR) by address lines and data lines (see Figure 5.12).

The I/O interface may be a part of the memory address space of the computer and may be accessed by the CPU in the same way as memory, except the CPU would be reading and writing to command and data registers of the interfaces such as disk drives, printers, and monitors (see Figure 5.12). Also some computers have separate I/O channels between the CPU and the I/O interfaces, that do not use the MAR and the MBR.

MAXnotes®

REA's Literature Study Guides

MAXnotes® are student-friendly. They offer a fresh look at masterpieces of literature, presented in a lively and interesting fashion. **MAXnotes®** offer the essentials of what you should know about the work, including outlines, explanations and discussions of the plot, character lists, analyses, and historical context. **MAXnotes®** are designed to help you think independently about literary works by raising various issues and thought-provoking ideas and questions. Written by literary experts who currently teach the subject, **MAXnotes®** enhance your understanding and enjoyment of the work.

Available **MAXnotes®** include the following:

Absalom, Absalom!
The Aeneid of Virgil
Animal Farm
Antony and Cleopatra
As I Lay Dying
As You Like It
The Autobiography of
    Malcolm X
The Awakening
Beloved
Beowulf
Billy Budd
The Bluest Eye, A Novel
Brave New World
The Canterbury Tales
The Catcher in the Rye
The Color Purple
The Crucible
Death in Venice
Death of a Salesman
The Divine Comedy I: Inferno
Dubliners
Emma
Euripides' Medea & Electra
Frankenstein
Gone with the Wind
The Grapes of Wrath
Great Expectations
The Great Gatsby
Gulliver's Travels
Hamlet
Hard Times

Heart of Darkness
Henry IV, Part I
Henry V
The House on Mango Street
Huckleberry Finn
I Know Why the Caged
    Bird Sings
The Iliad
Invisible Man
Jane Eyre
Jazz
The Joy Luck Club
Jude the Obscure
Julius Caesar
King Lear
Les Misérables
Lord of the Flies
Macbeth
The Merchant of Venice
The Metamorphoses of Ovid
The Metamorphosis
Middlemarch
A Midsummer Night's Dream
Moby-Dick
Moll Flanders
Mrs. Dalloway
Much Ado About Nothing
My Antonia
Native Son
1984
The Odyssey
Oedipus Trilogy

Of Mice and Men
On the Road
Othello
Paradise Lost
A Passage to India
Plato's Republic
Portrait of a Lady
A Portrait of the Artist
    as a Young Man
Pride and Prejudice
A Raisin in the Sun
Richard II
Romeo and Juliet
The Scarlet Letter
Sir Gawain and the
    Green Knight
Slaughterhouse-Five
Song of Solomon
The Sound and the Fury
The Stranger
The Sun Also Rises
A Tale of Two Cities
The Taming of the Shrew
The Tempest
Tess of the D'Urbervilles
Their Eyes Were Watching God
To Kill a Mockingbird
To the Lighthouse
Twelfth Night
Uncle Tom's Cabin
Waiting for Godot
Wuthering Heights

REA's Test Preps

The Best in Test Preparation

- REA "Test Preps" are far **more** comprehensive than any other test preparation series
- Each book contains up to **eight** full-length practice exams based on the most recent exams
- **Every** type of question likely to be given on the exams is included
- Answers are accompanied by **full** and **detailed** explanations

REA has published over 60 Test Preparation volumes in several series. They include:

Advanced Placement Exams (APs)
Biology
Calculus AB & Calculus BC
Chemistry
Computer Science
English Language & Composition
English Literature & Composition
European History
Government & Politics
Physics
Psychology
Spanish Language
United States History

**College Level Examination
~ Program (CLEP)**
American History I
Analysis & Interpretation of
    Literature
College Algebra
Freshman College Composition
General Examinations
Human Growth and Development
Introductory Sociology
Principles of Marketing

SAT II: Subject Tests
American History
Biology
Chemistry
French
German
Literature

SAT II: Subject Tests (continued)
Mathematics Level IC, IIC
Physics
Spanish
Writing

Graduate Record Exams (GREs)
Biology
Chemistry
Computer Science
Economics
Engineering
General
History
Literature in English
Mathematics
Physics
Political Science
Psychology
Sociology

ACT - American College Testing
    Assessment

ASVAB - Armed Service Vocational
    Aptitude Battery

CBEST - California Basic Educational
    Skills Test

CDL - Commercial Driver's License Exam

CLAST - College Level Academic Skills
    Test

ELM - Entry Level Mathematics

ExCET - Exam for Certification of
    Educators in Texas

FE (EIT) - Fundamentals of
    Engineering Exam

FE Review - Fundamentals of
    Engineering Review

GED - High School Equivalency
    Diploma Exam (US & Canadian
    editions)

GMAT - Graduate Management
    Admission Test

LSAT - Law School Admission Test

MAT - Miller Analogies Test

MCAT - Medical College Admission
    Test

MSAT - Multiple Subjects
    Assessment for Teachers

NTE - National Teachers Exam

PPST - Pre-Professional Skills Tests

PSAT - Preliminary Scholastic
    Assessment Test

SAT I - Reasoning Test

SAT I - Quick Study & Review

TASP - Texas Academic Skills
    Program

TOEFL - Test of English as a
    Foreign Language

RESEARCH & EDUCATION ASSOCIATION
61 Ethel Road W. • Piscataway, New Jersey 08854
Phone: (908) 819-8880

Please send me more information about your Test Prep Books

Name _____

Address _____

City _____ State _____ Zip _____

REA's **Problem Solvers**

The "PROBLEM SOLVERS" are comprehensive supplemental text-books designed to save time in finding solutions to problems. Each "PROBLEM SOLVER" is the first of its kind ever produced in its field. It is the product of a massive effort to illustrate almost any imaginable problem in exceptional depth, detail, and clarity. Each problem is worked out in detail with a step-by-step solution, and the problems are arranged in order of complexity from elementary to advanced. Each book is fully indexed for locating problems rapidly.

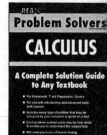

ACCOUNTING	HEAT TRANSFER
ADVANCED CALCULUS	LINEAR ALGEBRA
ALGEBRA & TRIGONOMETRY	MACHINE DESIGN
AUTOMATIC CONTROL	MATHEMATICS for ENGINEERS
SYSTEMS/ROBOTICS	MECHANICS
BIOLOGY	NUMERICAL ANALYSIS
BUSINESS, ACCOUNTING, & FINANCE	OPERATIONS RESEARCH
CALCULUS	OPTICS
CHEMISTRY	ORGANIC CHEMISTRY
COMPLEX VARIABLES	PHYSICAL CHEMISTRY
COMPUTER SCIENCE	PHYSICS
DIFFERENTIAL EQUATIONS	PRE-CALCULUS
ECONOMICS	PROBABILITY
ELECTRICAL MACHINES	PSYCHOLOGY
ELECTRIC CIRCUITS	STATISTICS
ELECTROMAGNETICS	STRENGTH OF MATERIALS &
ELECTRONIC COMMUNICATIONS	MECHANICS OF SOLIDS
ELECTRONICS	TECHNICAL DESIGN GRAPHICS
FINITE & DISCRETE MATH	THERMODYNAMICS
FLUID MECHANICS/DYNAMICS	TOPOLOGY
GENETICS	TRANSPORT PHENOMENA
GEOMETRY	VECTOR ANALYSIS

*If you would like more information about any of these books,
complete the coupon below and return it to us or visit your local bookstore.*

RESEARCH & EDUCATION ASSOCIATION
61 Ethel Road W. • Piscataway, New Jersey 08854
Phone: (908) 819-8880

Please send me more information about your Problem Solver Books

Name _____

Address _____

City _____ State _____ Zip _____